WITHDRAWN

ß/o1

Robert Herrick 1591-1674

By the same author

THE SWEDES, A JIGSAW PUZZLE

Robert Herrick
1591-1674

❧

GEORGE WALTON SCOTT

*Stay, stay
Untill the hasting day
Has run
But to the Even-song;
And, having pray'd together, we
Will goe with you along.*

St. Martin's Press
New York

Printed in Great Britain

To Maritta,
Philip, and Tom

Contents

List of Illustrations

9

We are grateful to the following for permission to reproduce the plates listed below : to the Leicester Museum and Art Gallery for plates 2, 3, 4; to the London Museum for plates 6, 7, 8, 10, 11; to the Greater London Council, as trustees of the Iveagh Bequest, Kenwood, for plate 9; to B. T. Batsford Limited for plate 15; to Crown Copyright, Ordnance Survey, for plate 19; to John R. Freeman, for plate 27; to the Faculty of Music, University of Oxford, for plate 28; to the Albertina, Vienna, for plate 29; to the National Portrait Gallery, for plate 30; to Thames and Hudson Limited, for plate 5; to Peter Dodd for plates 20–26.

Note
Unless otherwise indicated, all
quotations are from Herrick's
own verse

Preface

Nature as we have never seen

'To give us nature, such as we see it, is well and deserving of praise; to give us nature as we have never seen, but have often wished to see it, is better, and deserving of higher praise.' (Hazlitt : *On a Landscape of Nicholas Poussin*)

'. . . without Art, Nature can ne'er bee perfect : & without Nature, Art can clayme no being.' (Ben Jonson)

Much of what made Herrick the man is hidden from us and much of his life too is ghostly, as is the case of many other men and women of his period.

Lytton Strachey writing of the Elizabethans, the generation of Herrick's father, in *Elizabeth and Essex*, remarks on how the vacuum of time causes personalities to fade into figures without flesh and blood : 'More valuable than descriptions, but what perhaps is unattainable, would be some means by which the modern mind might reach to an imaginative comprehension of those beings three centuries ago . . . But the path seems closed to us. By what art are we to worm our way into those strange spirits, those even stranger bodies? The more clearly we perceive it, the more remote that singular universe becomes. With very few exceptions – possibly with the single exception of Shakespeare – the creatures in it meet us without intimacy; they are exterior visions, which we know, but do not truly understand.'

In certain lights, however, we can discern the man who looked out on the world around him : seventeenth-century London, Cambridge and the countryside of Devonshire.

Herrick had simple pious but untheological thoughts, a preoccupation with flowers, scents, clothing and precious stones, loved sack and was companionable. On the other hand, his love life is bleared by the shadow of convention, for his poems mostly reveal literary conceits rather than revelations of the heart.

Most important and relevant to a study of Herrick is his own inner world. This world remains bright and unclouded. It was a pastoral one which Hazlitt in his essay *On a Landscape of Nicholas Poussin* calls 'a happy noiseless dream', 'a suffusion of golden light', 'the world in its first naked glory, with the hues of fancy spread over it or in its high and palmy state'.

One of the neo-classical ideals of the Renaissance, Man's seeking of an ever-present and non-existent classical paradise, has been part of an ageless theme. The Sumerians looked back to a land that existed before the Flood. This 'dim Eden',[1] Arcadia for the Greeks, Eden for the Jews[2] exists too for many writers in a backward directed perspective to childhood.

Lord Clark in *Landscape into Art* describes this 'myth of ideal rusticity' which delighted Renaissance writers and painters as 'the most enchanting dream which has ever consoled mankind, the myth of a Golden Age in which man lived on the fruits of the earth, peacefully, piously and with primitive simplicity'.

The greatest exponents of this myth in painting were Giorgione and two near contemporaries of Herrick, Claude and Poussin. Herrick, like these painters, can recreate this classical landscape of Virgil to become another land equally vivid and newly fresh, elusive and serene. In the Campagna, Claude created a classical illusion far from reality. The actual place was a rocky landscape where peasants were ever struggling to make a bare living, working much of the time

1.   *Very old are we men*
                    Our dreams are tales
                    Told in dim Eden
                    By Eve's nightingales
            (3rd verse of Walter de la Mare's *All that's Past*)
2. The Christian and Jewish assumption was that not only had God once created a perfect world but also a perfect man and woman. Having sinned, the world sinned with them.

in intense heat. Herrick too escapes from the reality of early seventeenth-century England, one of the most restrictive periods in our economic history when a demand for wool produced a greater incentive to graze sheep rather than grow food, thus even producing starvation in some areas. His sole aim was to create pastoral masterpieces such as 'Corinna's Going a Maying'.

The increasing population[3] was creating pressure on the price of foodstuffs and a steady flow of people began leaving the land for the cities. At such a time pastoral poetry was a conceit devoid of reality, but this does not detract from its merits. Today we see the classicism of Herrick, itself second- and even third-hand, as a reflection in its own right. It can be admired as a backward look at the classical past. This glance is also suffused with the Christian heritage.

The next chapters will reflect Herrick the man and the outer world which he inhabited for over three quarters of a century.

3. The fall in population in Europe during the fourteenth-century was accelerated by the Black Death. It was not until about 1530 that it began to rise. The hundred years between 1530–1630 show a population explosion. There was then no major increase until the eighteenth-century.

1 His appearance

⌒∿⌒

There is only one portrait of Herrick extant. It depicts the poet
in middle age and it is by W. Marshall, who was also the
engraver of Bacon, Donne and Milton. It was placed before
the title page of *Hesperides* when it first appeared in 1648
(see pl. 1). Though perhaps a trifle flattering one can guess
there must be some likeness to the sitter since Herrick allowed
it to be published with the long prepared and much corrected
collection of his verse, but one suspects, too, that the engraver
has allowed the classical nature of the surroundings to enter
into his making of the poet's engraved effigy. Herrick's air in
this engraving is definitely Roman. But accept Marshall as his
portraitist Herrick did, and since other famous poets also
agreed to have their likenesses depicted by him, credence for a
reasonable resemblance to the original should be accepted.

The engraving shows little family likeness to the ancestral
portraits of the Herrick family now owned by the Leicester
Museum, but this is no proof of non-identity. The only
connexion between Marshall's portrait and the Herrick family
is oblique and rather humorous. Herrick's neck in the engraving
is bull-like, curiously analogous to the Herrick crest which is a
'bull's head argent'.

The profile shows a Roman nose, a keen lively eye sur-
mounted with strong black brows, a dark moustache, and a
rather up-turned chin. The hair is a thick mass of curls.

Herrick does mention in one of his poems that he has curly
hair.[1] There is in fact some information about his appearance
and condition in his verse. In another poem he says that he
has lost a finger :

1. 'On Himselfe'.

17

> *One of the five straight branches of my hand*
> *Is lopt already . . .*[2]

Written presumably when he was growing old, he tells of :

> *My uncontrolled brow*
> *And my retorted haires.*[3]

He records that he has become mop ey'd, near sighted,[4] and that his eyesight is waning.[5] It seems probable that he must have been nearly blind towards the very end of his life, isolated in his vicarage at Dean Prior in South Devon. He also describes his voice as weak.

His appearance in the Marshall engraving is robust and there is little doubt that he was strong and healthy. He came from a long-living family. His paternal grandmother, Mary Bond, lived to ninety-seven (see pl. 4), and left 142 children, grandchildren and great-grandchildren. Her husband, John Herrick, Herrick's grandfather, lived to seventy-six. Herrick's uncle Robert (see pl. 2), the first son of John Herrick and Mary Bond, lived to seventy-eight, and William Herrick (see pl. 3), the youngest son (and eleventh child) of John and Mary, lived to ninety-five. Herrick himself lived to eighty-three, an exceptionally great age for the period. He admits to being a hard drinker, and his life, though long sedentary while a parson secluded in the depths of the country, was not devoid of some deprivation and even hardship. Undoubtedly he had a good constitution.

2. 'Upon the losse of his Finger'.
3. 'To live merrily and to trust in good verses'.
4. 'Upon Himselfe'.
5. 'Upon his eye-sight failing him'.

2 Golden Cheapside

❧

The world which encompassed Herrick worked at a very leisured pace. It is difficult to imagine it today. The nearest approach to its tempo would be found in the country areas of present-day India.

One has to refer frequently to the obvious in order to recapture what it felt like to live at the time. As work was not dependent on machines men did not over-exert themselves and it was impossible for them to work at speed since they had a very long working day. There were, moreover, few incentives to work hard, so they worked in fits and starts, taking time off to speak to friends. The great majority, apart from those in such occupations as building, worked in their own houses. Builders in London started at five in the morning during summer and finished work at seven in the evening. Leaving out meal breaks they worked a seventy-five-hour week in summer, and a sixty-five-hour week in winter.

As in underdeveloped countries today there was a great deal of underemployment and probably most of the working people were labouring only half the year. Foreigners were under the impression that the English were lazy. One, Emanuel van Meteren, a Dutch merchant settled in London, wrote : 'The people are not so laborious and industrious as the Netherlanders or French, as they lead for the most part an indolent life like the Spaniards . . . the most toilsome, difficult, and skilful works are chiefly performed by foreigners, as among the idle Spaniards.'

The better-off, too, lived at what we would consider a very leisurely pace, and they enjoyed few comforts as we understand them. Communications were very slow indeed (so rumour was rampant); the arrival of posts was often long delayed. This

20

slowness had its advantages for, though life in towns was bustling, there was none of the pressure on the lives of towns-people which the city-dweller of today experiences.

Existence thus had a static quality and men, though the world was opening to them, had not yet conceived the idea of progress. Every man with any pretence to learning, wrote. Many played instruments.

On the other hand, they were constantly confronted with death through insanitary conditions, and they were liable to leave this life suddenly on the scaffold, in the back streets, on the highways and on battlefields. The world was not a safe place and comforts were rare—many lived in abject poverty, crowded into rooms of ramshackle houses—but the English were a young, dynamic people.

Herrick was born in Cheapside in 1591 and was later apprenticed as a goldsmith to his uncle in Wood Street nearby. The Goldsmith's Row where he was born of Nicholas and Julian was on the south side of the street only a few paces from Bow Church. If ever the hackneyed definition of a Cockney were correct, Herrick was a true Londoner, for the Bow bells could be heard clearly in the house where he was born.

'Golden Cheapside',[1] as Herrick called it, was broader than it is now, probably twice its present breadth. It had long been the principal market place of London (Chepe – O.E. ceap, market – means a bargain). Its houses were of black and white timber. Often each storey projected above the lower one, giving a top heavy appearance like that of old galleons. Cheapside was more of a market place than a thoroughfare, with a great number of stalls and tables arranged along its centre, from St Paul's to the Carfax, selling all kinds of merchandise from live peacocks to the small turnips which grew in the village of Hackney and were brought to the area near the Eleanor Cross by the village women. Stationers were situated near the Cross at the end of Wood Street. The space between Gutter Lane and Foster Lane was often called the 'Cartes in Chepe' since it was a place where carts bringing bread to the City from Stratford were placed. Shops and taverns stretched between

1. *Or to the* Golden-Cheap-side, *where my earth*
    Of Julia Herrick *gave to me my Birth.*
    'His tears to Thamasis'

21

Bow Lane and Queen Street. These were followed by the Pelltry (skinners, tailors and ironmongers) and two shops opposite the end of Milk Street called the Cow and the Milkmaid.

The taverns were numerous and included the Nag's Head, the Cardinal's Hat, the Mermaid and the Half Moon.

The salesmanship was high-powered. The salesmen and women came from all parts of London and the adjoining countryside. Pilfering and thieving were rampant and a large part of the criminal community was made up from the *canaille* that frequented St Paul's Cathedral.

Cheapside was the very centre of London and it was very noisy. Apart from the calls of the street vendors there were the cries of such itinerant salesmen as the water carriers, with a high reputation for gossip, who bore fresh water from house to house. The conduit of West Cheap was the principal source of water supply in the market and drew it not from the Thames but from the heights of rural Paddington. To the north of Cheapside and the Poultry one was confronted with the harsh noise of the lathes of the metal founders turning out such merchandise as candlesticks and spice mortars. Cheapside was one of the few really wide streets in London and here for a long time past the stalls were cleared away for a joist or an execution. Here goods too badly-made were publicly burned. All great land processions passed along it, monarchs on their way from the tower to be crowned at Westminster, foreign kings and queens, ambassadors and returning heroes. On such occasions crowds cheered from the street itself while the families of the merchants packed their windows which were decorated with hanging tapestries, gold and silver cloths and wreaths of flowers.

In his *Survey of London*, Stow describes Herrick's actual birthplace in some detail :

> Next to be noted, the most beautiful frame of fayre houses and shoppes, that bee within the Walles of London, or else where in England, commonly called Goldsmithes Rowe, betwixt Bredstreet end & the Crosse in Cheape, but is within this Bredstreete warde, the same was builded by *Thomas Wood* Goldsmith, one of the shiriffes of London, in the yeare 1491. It contayneth in number tenne fayre dwelling houses,

and fourteene shoppes, all in one frame, vniformely builded foure stories high, bewtified towards the streete with the Golsmithes armes and the likeness of woodmen, in memory of his name, riding on monstruous beasts, all which is cast in lead, richly painted ouer and gilt, these gaue to the Goldsmithes with stockes of money to be lent to yong men, hauing those shops &c. This saide Front was againe new painted and guilt over, in the yeare 1594. Sir Richard Martin being then Mayor, and keeping his Mayoralty in one of them, seruing out the time of Cutbert Buckle from the second of July, till the 28. of October. [Text of 1603.]

Goldsmith's Row was the true pride of Cheapside. When Herrick was born, residence was restricted to goldsmiths. Then it contained fourteen shops loaded with gold and silver. It was later in 1620 that 'meaner trades' such as milliners, linen drapers and booksellers began to move into the buildings.

Very near Goldsmith's Row, in the middle of Cheapside, stood the famous Cheapside Cross. For the Elizabethan Londoner it represented what Eros in Piccadilly Circus does today. It was one of the series of twelve memorial crosses erected by Edward I to mark the stages in the funeral procession of his queen, Eleanor of Castile, from Lincolnshire to her tomb at Westminster. It bore the arms of England and the queen's own native Castile and Leon. Three years after Herrick's birth it was gilded and renovated but its statues were broken by zealots and hooligans. It remained a battered monument with its gilded apex until it was finally destroyed by the Puritans in 1643. A fragment of the Cheapside Cross remains in the Guildhall Museum.

Herrick was baptized on 24 August 1591 in the parish church of St Vedast in Foster Lane (three years after the defeat of the Spanish Armada). Here his six older brothers and sisters had been christened before him. His uncle Robert was godfather.

St Vedast still stands, renovated after the Blitz. It was newly built at the beginning of the sixteenth century and was repaired and enlarged in 1614. It was not entirely destroyed during the Fire and its tower stood till 1694. In Herrick's time it was situated at the extreme western end of Cheapside where Foster Lane ran into the thoroughfare before the fork into a small lane, Blow Bladder Street. The fork on the opposite side of Cheapside led to St Paul's.

St Vedast was one of the thirteen peculiars – the name given to thirteen churches of which Bow Church was the principal. Exempt from the jurisdiction of the Bishop of London, they came under the authority of the Archbishop of Canterbury.

The Herricks were from Leicestershire. The name is of Scandinavian origin and it is spelt in different ways: Erick, Heyrick, Herrick etc. It was not aspirated in writing until the end of the sixteenth century. People with the name of Herrick are fairly common in the eastern part of the county. The family was established about the year 1300. They are believed to have come into Leicester from the nearby village of Houghton towards the end of the fifteenth century. It was not long before they became prominent as tradesmen and as members of the Corporation.[2]

The connexion with Houghton continued for a very long period however. Robert Herrick's great-grandfather Thomas Eyrick moved from the village to the town during the reign of Henry VIII. By this time they were very well established and bore a coat of arms. The descendants of the poet's uncle Robert lived and owned property at Houghton until the end of the eighteenth century. Two of them became Town Clerks of the City of Leicester. The Herricks of Beaumanor were the descendants of Robert's uncle Sir William Herrick. The line died out in 1876 with William Perry Herrick but his widow survived in possession of the estate until 1915 since when it passed under William Perry Herrick's will to successive members of the Curzon family who have assumed the name Herrick. All the land has now been sold.

Thomas's second son John (d. 1589) was Robert's grandfather. He was twice Mayor of Leicester and started the family business of ironmongery which was to flourish in their hands

2. Apart from Robert, the Herrick family also produced another great writer: the author of *Gulliver's Travels*. Swift's father married a Mrs Abigail Erick. In his *Fragment of Autobiography* (1667–99) Swift writes that the Ericks 'derive their lineage from Erick the forester, a great commander, who raised an army to oppose the invasion of William the Conqueror, by whom he was vanquished, but afterward employed to command that prince's forces; and in his old age retired to his house in Leicestershire, where his family hath continued ever since, but declining every age, and are now in the condition of very private gentlemen.'

for one hundred years. He married Mary Bond of Ward End, Warwickshire, and they raised a large and notable family. Herrick's father, Nicholas, was their second son. He was interested in metals but wished to become a goldsmith. There was none of this trade in Leicester so he migrated to London and lived in Goldsmith's Row. In a time when the merchant classes were rising to greater power and social prestige, he completed a successful apprenticeship and eventually became a goldsmith and banker of some standing.

In 1582 he married Julian, Juliana, or Julia, daughter of William Stone, a London mercer (part of their business was specifically for goldsmiths), and they produced eight children. The eldest William died young and the youngest, also William, was born posthumous to his father.[3]

The baptisms of seven of the children were recorded in the register of St Vedast: William, 1585, Martha, January 1586, Mercie, December 1586, Thomas, 1588, Nicholas, 1589, Ann, 1590, Robert, 24 August 1591.

Herrick's father Nicholas made his will on 7 November 1592: "In the name of God Amen The Seaventh Daye of November A thousand ffive hundredth ninety twoe I Nicholas Herricke goldsmith of perfecte memorye in sowle but sicke in bodye Doe make and ordayne this my Last will and testament . . ."

The will was witnessed by his unmarried brother, William, and his married sister, Helen Holden. He estimated that he possessed about £3,000, leaving the third part to his wife Julian and the rest equally to his six children then alive.

Two days later tragedy struck. Nicholas fell from the fourth floor of his house into the road and died. Whether this was an accident or a suicide is not known. He was buried at St Vedast's on the tenth.

Suicides were rare in the sixteenth century but in this case

3. Evidently Robert became very close to his younger brother. Long afterwards he wrote a poem *To his dying Brother, Master William Herrick*:

> *Life of my life, take not so soone thy flight,*
> *But stay the time till we have bade good night . . .*

and

> *Love is most loathe to leave the thing beloved . . .*

it was suspected, and as a suicide's goods reverted to the crown, an inquiry was at once set up by the Bishop of Bristol, the Queen's High Almoner, Dr Richard Fletcher (the father of the dramatist).

The Almoner's statement ran as follows :

And where one Nich'as Herrick late citezeine and Goldsmythe of London about the Nyneth daye of this instant moneth of November (as is supposed) did throwe himself forthe of a garret window in London aforesaide whereby he did kill and destroye himself, By reason whereof all such goodes chattells and debtes as were the said Nich'as Herrickes at the tyme of his deathe or ought any waies to apperteyne or belonge vnto him do nowe belonge apperteyne and are forfeyted vnto O^r said sou'aigne Lady the quene by force of her P'rogatyve royall and nowe are in the only order and disposicon of me the saide bushopp Almoner in augmentacon of her moste gracious almes by force and vertue of the said l'res patentes to me made and graunted as aforesaide (if the saide Nich'as Herrick be or shalbe founde felon of himselfe). [*Miscellanea Genealogica et Heraldica*, ed. J. J. Howard, 2nd series, vol. i, p. 40.]

On 13 November the Lords of the Council wrote to the Lord Mayor of London not to allow the coroner to pronounce a verdict in the case of Nicholas Herrick until there had been a thorough investigation into the cause of his death.

Julian Herrick, pregnant, with six children (Robert then the youngest, only one year three months), must have certainly been afflicted with grief and anxiety, but there was some hope for her welfare in that through her own relatives and the Herricks she had connexions with people of influence in London. Giles, her brother-in-law, was the City Secretary. Another brother-in-law, William, was a man of some substance who had been sent on a mission to Turkey and was held in good favour at Court. Mary Herrick had married Thomas Bennet, later Lord Mayor of London. Of Julian's own family, the Stones, her brother was a well-known lawyer and her sister Ann had married into a prominent family of influence, the Soanes.

Within the month, on 29 November, the Almoner renounced claim in his report on the inquiry to the goods of Nicholas Herrick, 'being moved wth charity and for dyvers other good causes' and 'consideracons'. The question of suicide had not yet been cleared, but the estate would be granted to Julian and her children according to the will. Herrick later wrote a poem 'To the reverend[4] shade of his religious Father' in which he writes

> . . . *Forgive, forgive me; since I did not know*
> *Whether thy bones had here their Rest, or no . . .*

which could be interpreted to mean that it was still not advisable to let the exact place where he was buried be known, since the question of suicide was still in abeyance.

The estate was in fact worth £5,068, more than Nicholas had estimated. Its administration was entrusted to an alderman, Sir Richard Martin, Nicholas's brother, William, and the Almoner's brother, Giles Fletcher.

It appears that Julian Herrick must have had some property of her own as she made over her share of the will to the children so that the six would inherit about £800 each.

Her two brothers-in-law, Robert and William, were named in Nicholas's will as 'overseers', or advisers to the executors, and Letters of Administration were granted, in the minority of the two executors, to Robert on 13 February 1592/3. Robert was a prosperous iron merchant from Leicester. He was three times Lord Mayor of the town and our poet's godfather. William had gone to London about 1574 as an apprentice to Herrick's father, and he later became a goldsmith in his own right. He was very successful and rented the estate of Beaumanor in Leicester; he became a knight in 1605.

There could not have been two better executors of the will. Robert and William both liked each other and they were conscientious. It was a time of intense inflation which hit the peasantry hard while the gentry, the professions and the merchant classes tended to gain by it. One can guess that the money left in the will was well invested. Twenty years after

4. To revere had the meaning at this time of being reluctant to do something through a feeling of respect.

these events, William wrote to Robert that a letter from him was as welcome as eighteen trumpeters.

*   *

The early life of Herrick is one of those periods in his existence in which practically nothing about him is recorded and he remains ghostly to us.

Nichols[5] records a tradition that the youngest child in the family, William,[6] was born at Hampton-on-Thames at the home of Julian's married sister Anne Campion, and that Julian had gone there to live as the plague was raging in London. F. W. Moorman in his biography of Herrick (1912 and 1915) and Emily Easton in *Youth Immortal* (1934) concluded that Julian lived there some time with the Campion family and that Robert was thus brought up in the country. There is no solid evidence for this and where he passed his infancy is not known.

There were many relations who could have come to the aid of the stricken family. On his father's side there were four aunts and uncles in London and seven in Leicester. Marchette Chute in *Two Gentle Men* (1960) conjectures that Robert, as the poet's godfather, having special responsibility for his small namesake took him to live with his wife and eleven children in their large house in Leicester. Here again one is in the realm of speculation.

It is also unknown where he went to school though some of his biographers have asserted that he attended Hampton Grammar School or Westminster, but there is no tangible evidence for these surmises.

Wherever he went to school, it is certain that like any other child of the time he received what today would be considered a sound classical education and like other Elizabethan or Jacobean children had to work a very long day. A grammar school in Leicester, for instance, worked the boys six days a week for twelve hours in summer from 5 a.m. to 5 p.m. Six hours of Cicero, Caesar or Virgil before lunch and four hours again in the afternoon was not uncommon.

5. John Nichols, *The History and Antiquities of the County of Leicester*.
6. There was a custom during this period to use again the name of an older child that had died.

It is also known that from 1594–7, when Herrick was aged between three and six, summer followed summer with constant rain. The corn stood green in the fields, the meadows were soaked, the cattle perished and with them many people.

Herrick is probably referring to a time after the year 1597 when he writes with great delight in 'His Tears to Thamasis' of going to bathe 'in the summers sweeter evenings' in his 'silver-footed Thamasis' and of gliding in 'Barge (with boughes and rushes beautifi'd) to Richmond, Kingstone, and to Hampton-Court', 'Landing here, or safely Landing there' on his way to his 'Beloved Westminster' or Cheapside.

The next concrete fact recorded of Herrick's life is his apprenticeship to his uncle, Sir William Herrick, who is described as being 'remarkably handsome and of great abilities and address'.

3   The Apprentice

The contention of some of his critics, based on the statement by Nichols that Herrick's understanding of nature must have been generated by an early life spent in country surroundings, is contradicted not only by a lack of real evidence but also by the character of London itself. The country was never far away. Though London more than doubled its population during Elizabeth's reign, nowhere, not even in the centre of the City at Cheapside, was a man far from a landscape of open fields with few hedges, manor houses, and windmills. Middlesex still lay uncleared of its old forest and the citizen could go hunting in the woods of Hampstead and Highgate.

On the Surrey side of the Thames the country came even nearer to the town. The theatres and bear-pits practically abutted on to fields. Gerard looked along the banks of the Thames for specimens for his Herball. The movement from London into the countryside was continuous. Many Londoners went hawking on the outskirts of their city and the city musters were held at Moorfields and Finsbury Fields. Here too the train-bands drilled and practised shooting at the butts. Herb gatherers would pick their merchandise under the hedges of what is now Piccadilly.

The landscape was green right up to the city boundaries except where the suburbs had grown along the highways leading out from the capital.

Herrick could have walked westwards from St Paul's towards Holborn, and by the time he had reached St Giles's Church, which stood on what is now Shaftesbury Avenue, he would be in fields.

To the north of Cheapside, if a traveller passed through Cripplegate (accompanied if he were wise, for he could easily

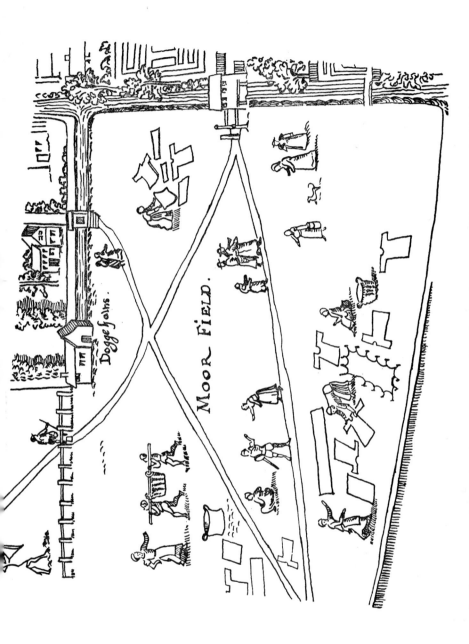

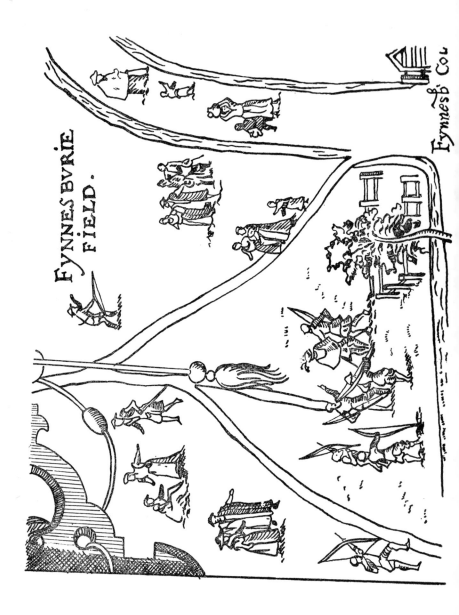

be waylaid), he would only have about twenty minutes' walk through the suburbs and he would see the countryside of Middlesex rising up directly before him. Soon, too, he would arrive at one of the homesteads which supplied the city with its food. Here, if in the right season, he might easily take part in a sheep-shearing celebration. But a traveller would also be confronted with bad roads on the outskirts that turned into quagmires when it rained and here, too, he would have to be wary of sudden violence. Violence, like the countryside, was never far away.

From most parts of London a man might see flocks of wild duck or teal flying above him on their way from the marshes in the north to the river marshes on the south bank between Paris Garden and Lambeth.

He would also be constantly aware of nature even nearer at hand, for the large gardens which adjoined most ancient houses were well stocked with fruit trees. These dwellings were laid out with large beds where flowers were grown 'to furnish the chambers'.

The spectacle of sixteenth- and early seventeenth-century England is bright and alive from the works of the poets, dramatists and writers of all types of literature, but it is worth remembering once again that our own tempo and the availability of immediate communication isolate us from its leisurely haphazard existence. Machinery was restricted to such simple devices as the water mill and the windmill. Power came from animals and skills were wielded by hand. There were few clocks so Londoners had little sense of time. In the afternoon most people would take a siesta. Life started early. Streets were full of people soon after dawn and the alehouses were open to their customers. It was a slow-moving, for us a timeless world.

A young apprentice was confronted with an enchanting, quite cosmopolitan town but it was certainly no idyll. Life was fraught with dangers. Some districts, such as Alsatia, one entered at one's own peril.

London at this period was still essentially a medieval cathedral city, rising behind its walls. Its gates shut each night when darkness came.

It was not a quiet place. The streets were cobbled and

coaches and carts rumbled loudly as they passed. Vendors shouted in the streets and the apprentices bawled their wares at passers-by. There was a great deal of music to be heard from the singing cries of sellers to the voices and instruments of the wits and gallants of the Inns of Court, the 'Third University', who rivalled each other in voice when crossing the river to the south bank for a night's entertainment.

The skyline was silhouetted by the spires and bell towers of one hundred and nine churches. The custom of bell ringing had increased in the seventeenth century. On certain occasions such as a monarch's progress down-river to Greenwich, there was a deep, widely flung and various chiming of bells by order of the Court. During a funeral bells could ring for as long as six hours.

Outside the city, the country lay silent except for the occasional church bell, the sound of animals or human voices heard at a distance.

Many of the overlapping London houses carried gilded signs that hung from their iron frames – grasshoppers, silver luces, hedgehogs and flower pots. Then there were the innumerable inn signs : swans, bears, coats of arms, sea monsters, mermaids and nags' heads.

Smells were everywhere – the stink of unwashed human beings, of wines, beers and spirits and tobacco from the taverns, of fruit, vegetables, meat and fish from the markets, and smoke from the open fires.

A mile or more from the City of London stood the royal city of Westminster, Herrick called it '*my Beloved Westminster*', where the King held court and Parliament assembled.

The lighting of London was a duty enforced on the citizens themselves until 1661. People were required to hang out candles or lamps when nights were dark. For the most part tallow candles were the chief means of lighting.

In the evening when the sun had set, most of the real din ceased. Voices spoke from out of the darkness and the taverns sounded in the narrow streets with songs, chatter and shouts. When the noises ceased the night grew dark and calm. The lights were finally put out. The glazed windows of the rich no longer shone bright, and slats of the wooden lattices of the less wealthy no longer threw out shafts of yellow. The night watchman's call told the citizens of London to look to their clocks, fires and lights.

This was the world surrounding Herrick in his youth. Its effect was profound. When for long periods throughout his life he was away from London he was to regret his absence from his native city deeply.

There were two main glories which Londoners boasted. The river, Herrick's *silver-footed Thamasis*, and St Paul's Cathedral. The Thames was the city's main thoroughfare in whose unpolluted water salmon and sturgeon were caught. John Taylor, 'the Water Poet', said that two thousand small boats were to be found about the river. One penny was charged as a ferry fare from the north to the south bank and up to sixpence was asked for journeys from east to west. These fees were regulated over a period of fifty years but the boat owners asked to be tipped heavily and they would hurl abuse at any passenger if they thought they were being tipped short. Many of these boatmen were old sailors who had fought against the Armada and had been on voyages to the Indies.

The briskest trade was from the north to the south bank. It is believed that from three to four thousand people crossed daily by this route. They were mostly return passengers seeking pleasure in the theatres and bear-pits of the Bankside and Paris Garden. It was a journey Herrick, as an apprentice, must have made frequently for the apprentices were traditionally an important and vociferous sector of the theatre audiences.

In contrast to the bustle of the smaller public craft the large elegant barges of the Court could be seen gliding along the water on special state occasions.

On both sides of the river, to the east of London Bridge, that other great thoroughfare to the south with its conglomeration of shops and dwellings, lived the sailors, ship victuallers and purveyors. It was here that a Londoner could hear of the world beyond his city : of Europe, Asia and the Americas.

The other pride of London was Old St Paul's built during the twelfth and thirteenth centuries, 520 feet from the ground to the top of its steeple, but in Herrick's time rather less high since its steeple had been destroyed by lightning. Its huge size dominated the city and Londoners thought of it as a symbol of immortality.

During this period the benches at the door of the Choir were used by beggars and drunkards. The Middle Aisle was known as St Paul's Walk where between 11 a.m. and 2 p.m. and again at 6 p.m. all classes of society gathered. The cathedral, too, was the meeting place for brokers, usurers, the poor, pimps and prostitutes. On its pillars notices for the hire of servants were posted. A large part of the building was in shockingly bad repair during Herrick's early life. No reparation of any scale was carried out until the year 1633, during the reign of Charles I.

Standing at the western end of Cheapside the cathedral and its yard formed with the thoroughfare the very centre of London. The churchyard covered an area of twelve and a half acres and was roughly rectangular, though it was narrower at the west than at the east. Houses and shops were built against the precinct walls. Many of the shops were booksellers and printers and stationers, for St Paul's Churchyard and Paternoster Row together with a few outlying bookshops in Fleet Street by St Dunstan's Church formed the literary quarters of London. Bookshops were then (as they were even as late as the early part of Victoria's reign) the meeting place for scholars, divines, poets and students.

Herrick must have spent much of his early manhood in the area and it was here in 1648 that he was to supervise the printing of *Hesperides*.

The central point of the churchyard was St. Paul's Cross where Londoners throughout the ages had crowded to hear proclamations of state edicts. It was from here on 20 August 1588 that the Dean of St Paul's made the first public announcement of the defeat of the Spanish Armada. In 1595 (Herrick was then four) St Paul's Cross (see pl. 12) was repaired and partly enclosed by a low brick wall. Along the eastern wall of the precincts stood St Paul's School, founded in 1509 by Colet.

The year 1607 saw the beginning of the partnership of Beaumont and Fletcher (which lasted until 1613). During his apprenticeship Herrick must have seen their plays as well as those of a man whose works were later to be a great influence on his writing, Ben Jonson (*The Alchemist* appeared in 1610).

The winter of 1607 saw the Great Frost which set in during

December and continued for seven weeks. Stalls were placed on the frozen Thames. There was much skating and on one occasion youths burned a gallon of wine upon the ice.

Apart from training his apprentice, the master took on the responsibility for the young man's welfare, so the link between Herrick and his uncle was a close one. William had been apprenticed to his elder brother, Herrick's own father, and so he now had the opportunity to return the care and the training he himself had gained. This is the indenture of the apprentice-ship:

This indenture witnesseth that Robert Herick the sonne of Nicholas Herick of London, Goldsmithe, doth put him selfe apprentize to Sir Wm. Herick, Knighte, citizen, and goldsmith of London to learnee his Arte. And with him (after the manner of Apprentize) to serve from the feaste of St Bartholomew the apostle last past before the date heereof unto the full end and terme of Tenn yeres from thence next following to be full complete and ended. During which terme the said Apprentize his said master faithfully shall serve his secrets keepe his lawfull commandements every where gladly doe. He shall doe no damage to his said master, nor see to be done of other but that so his power shall lett, or forthwith give warning to his master of the same. He shall not waste the goode of his said master nor lend them unlawfully to any p.son : He shall not commit fornication nor contract matrimony within the said terme. He shall not playe at cardes, dice, tables or any other unlawfull games whereby his said master may have any losse with his own goode or others during the said terme without licence of his said master; he shall neither beg nor stele : he shall not haunt Tavernes nor absent him selfe from his said master's service daie nor nighte unlawfully. But in all thinges as a faithfull Apprentize he shall behave him selfe towards his said master and all his during the said terme. And the said master his said Apprentize in the same Arte which he useth, by the best means he can, shall teach and instruct with due correction, finding unto his said Apprentize meate, drinke, Apparell, Lodging, and all other necessaries according to the Custome of the Citty of London during the said terme. And for the true performance of all and singuler the said covenants and agreements either of the saide parties bindeth him selfe unto the other by theis presents. In witness whereof the parties above named to this Indenture interchangably have put their hand and seales the XXVth daie of September in the year of our Lord God 1607, and in ffyfte yere of the Raigne of our Soveraigne Lord King James, by the grace of God King of England Scotland ffrance and Ireland, defender of the ffaith etc.

[signed] Robert Herricke

[dated Sept 25th 1607]

The vows of sobriety made by an apprentice to his master were not usually kept : apprentices were very unruly. Frederick Duke of Wirtemberg visiting London in 1592 observed that no foreigner dare cross to the opposite side of the street if apprentices were collected together there in crowds. They struck to left and right without mercy. 'Clubs' was the rallying cry of the 'hopefuls' as they were called. This cry meant trouble.

Under the law the apprentice lived in the master's house almost as a son. In such conditions Herrick must have been eager to do credit to his dead father and please his living uncle.

When Robert came to live with his uncle and his wife Joan in Wood Street (off Cheapside), six of their twelve children had been born. One was named Robert and another Henry at the request of Prince Henry (who became Prince of Wales in 1610).

At this time Sir William Herrick owned land in thirteen counties and had homes both in Richmond and Westminster, apart from Wood Street. He served Leicester in Parliament and was known as 'the town's special good friend'. William bought Beaumanor which belonged formerly to the Earl of Essex in 1598 and became Lord of Barrow, Woodhouse, Quorndon, Woodthorpe and Mountsorrel. His tenants had to bring him 'one red-rose garland' on Midsummer's Day and fat turkeys and claret at Christmas. He had deer in his park and fish in his moat and also the right to keep his own swans marked with his initials on the River Stour. His brother Robert developed an orchard for him with peach and pear from his own grounds and reported to him on the timber and game during his absence.

It would thus appear that Herrick did not spend all his time at Wood Street, or indeed in London. He must have moved from house to house with his uncle's family, at least occasionally. There were twenty-seven public holidays a year since the passing of a bill in 1552 including a long period of leisure at Christmas, killed by the Puritans in the middle of the seventeenth century. There also existed the festivals of the Lord of Misrule, similar to the feast of Ceres in Rome. During some of these festivals and holidays the family must have moved from Wood Street to one of the other dwellings.

For his initiation as an apprentice Herrick and his uncle went to Goldsmith's Hall, a short distance from Wood Street, near Foster Lane[1]. Here his name was entered in the books and he presented his signed indenture to the Master and the Wardens.

The company had pleasant gardens and a courtyard. The building itself had a magnificent bay window with armorial bearings, possessed Flemish tapestries depicting the life of the patron saint of goldsmiths, Saint Dunstan, and a silver-gilt and jewelled image of the saint in the hall.

The Goldsmiths also had the oversight of chantries of a number of churches including Herrick's christening place, St Vedast, for the livery companies were part economic and part religious and adopted a parish church as their religious home. The Goldsmith's Company maintained 'St Dunstan's light' in the church of St John Zachary, and had a chapel dedicated to him and containing his image at St Paul's.

The average apprenticeship for a goldsmith in London lasted seven years. This period of time could be shortened by special arrangement if the apprentice was related to his master, but as is stated in the indenture, Sir William Herrick evidently felt that Robert should serve a full ten years. A goldsmith's art and skill were difficult to acquire.

The luxury trades were divided into two grades. In the higher

1. 'On the east side of Foster Lane, at the Engayne end is the Goldsmith's Hall, a proper house, but not large'. Stow: *Survey of London*. (It was enlarged in 1634–6 and badly damaged by the Fire in 1666).

grade were the goldsmiths who were the most experienced and skilled and the jewellers were the lesser. The goldsmiths covered the shrines of kings and saints with golden tracery and figurines studded with jewels and enamels, made bishops' mitres, covered the sacred books of the church, and made buckles, girdles, salt cellars, spoons and other fine objects.

His apprenticeship brought Herrick into contact with the social and quite probably the literary world of early seventeenth-century London. In a good business such as his uncle's he would get to know the principal courtiers and men of influence of England.

His uncle in fact 'resided constantly at court', had been in Queen Elizabeth's confidence and now had the ear of James I. 'By honourable services to both [he] acquired a large property.'

Although differences in income were immense, it was not an age of social exclusiveness, and people of different backgrounds were brought together by common interests. The relationship between the patron and the protégé seemed to be perfectly natural to the subjects of Elizabeth and James. Social snobbery developed much later in this country.

It was very probably during this time as an apprentice goldsmith that he cultivated a close-eyed view of the world and a taste for minuteness, but his interest in small objects was also natural to a myopic. He writes of children, robins, grasshoppers and beads, and uses such diminutives as youngling, kitling and quarelets.

The materials of the goldsmith's trade appear in much of his verse. The convention of comparing his mistress's features to precious stones was not an unusual one for a poet of the time, but with Herrick one easily detects a close familiarity with the symbols he chooses:

'The Rock of Rubies : and The quarrie of Pearls'

Some ask'd me where the Rubies *grew?*
And nothing I did say:
But with my finger pointed to
The lips of Julia.
Some ask'd how Pearls *did grow, and where?*

Then spoke I to my Girle,
To part her lips, and shew'd them there
The Quarelets of Pearl.

It is during this period of his life as an apprentice that Herrick's earliest poems can be dated. The first known poem that can be dated approximately was written in *c.* 1610 at the age of nineteen. It is to his brother Thomas, on his leaving London to farm in Leicestershire. This poem depicts the classical ideal of the life of an English gentleman and the virtues of a simple country existence. The influence of Ben Jonson can be seen, for it is similar to the older poet's address 'To Sir Robert Wroth'. It also has many classical sources and some of the classical imagery is unintentionally comic. It is unlikely for instance that his brother would rise in the morning to sacrifice to Jove. In the poem Herrick is delightfully frank about the impression made on him by his new sister-in-law Elizabeth (very possibly the Elizabeth who kept house for him late in life when he was a clergyman at Dean Prior in Devonshire), whom he refers to as 'not so beautifull, as chast'.

It is a poem of considerable merit, particularly considering he wrote it at an early age. It contains many charming passages as :

And the brisk Mouse may feast her selfe with crums
Till the green-ey'd kitling comes.

Thomas had been apprenticed to a merchant named Massam who in 1610 was paid off by Sir William, acting as banker, so that he could leave London to marry Elizabeth Stanford.

Another poem which can be dated before 1612 was 'To my dearest Sister M. Mercie Herrick' who was five years older than Herrick. She married John Wingfield at Little Thurlow in Suffolk in 1611. Wingfield was a graduate of Cambridge who was later admitted to Gray's Inn, and knighted in 1619. An early poem is also addressed to him : 'To his Brother in Law Master John Wingfield' :

For being comely, consonant, and free
To most of men, but most of all to me . . .

The departure of his brother Thomas to Leicestershire to start a completely new life as a farmer, and his sister Mercie's leaving for Suffolk may well have led Herrick to question his own future vocation as a goldsmith. Perhaps, too, doubts about his future career were also even more deeply implanted in his mind by the realization that he wrote good verse. Very likely he was already acquainted with some of the poets of the day and his interests were being directed elsewhere.

By the year 1613, at the age of twenty-two, it was very plain to him that he did not ever want to wear the violet and scarlet livery of the Goldsmith's Company. With four years of apprenticeship still to run Herrick was released from his contract by his uncle and it was decided that he would go up to Cambridge.

4   The Fellow-commoner

Cambridge University at this time was a microcosm of English society, for it took its students from all walks of life. That society was based on a special sense of freedom, not the freedom of equality, but on the idea of freedom of opportunity. People mixed freely. The classes themselves changed with the acquisition of property, and some individuals moved haphazardly up and down the social ladder with considerable flexibility. To an extent universities were areas of social mobility although movement took place for the most part at the top sections of the social scale. Undergraduates came from the nobility and the squirearchy. Many were the sons of poor parsons, farmers, tailors, shoemakers, inn-keepers, blacksmiths, labourers and those described as 'plebians'. The poor students and the sizars acted as valets to the wealthier students, cleaning their boots and dressing their hair. They did not consider these duties in any way as chores beneath their dignity, nor did they perform them with any reluctance. Differences of position were taken as a matter of course. There was not a great deal of envy or jealousy on the part of the less fortunate for the more fortunate. It was not until the eighteenth century that the 'grand law of subordination' was taught to the 'inferior orders'.

The grammar schools took the cleverest boys from all classes. They were brought up together and many went to Oxford and Cambridge. The course of study comprised the study of the Classics and of Rhetoric and Logic. The language of the colleges and of instruction was Latin, for Latin was the language of literature, of religion (an inheritance of the Church of Rome) and of diplomacy. By the strict rules of the statutes of Queen Elizabeth, students were required to use Latin, Greek or Hebrew everywhere in conversation except in their rooms. By the time Herrick was at Cambridge, however, there was a tendency for these regulations to be waived.

Herrick, unlike Ben Jonson, was certainly no erudite scholar, but it was inevitable that from his schooldays to his leaving university, and also in later life, the worlds of Ancient Greece and Rome constantly permeated his thoughts.

Herrick became a fellow-commoner of St John's in the summer of 1613 at the age of twenty-two. He was well above the average age of undergraduates who generally came to Cambridge at sixteen (some were even thirteen or fourteen). Although older than most students he could not have felt a real gap in age as people at that time developed early. At sixteen or at the latest at seventeen you were a man. A girl was a woman at fourteen. The status of fellow-commoner was mostly designed for the sons of wealthy families who paid double fees. Herrick thus enjoyed privileges such as dining on the dais in the College Hall.

St John's had its own walks, bowling green and royal tennis court. A pleasant enough place, it had reached a low state of learning but enjoyed a high reputation for drinking, to which the author of 'The Welcome to Sack' and other poems would have little difficulty in conforming. He wrote of strong wine :

> *Thou mak'st me ayrie, active to be born, . . .*

and

> *Swell up my nerves with spirit; let my blood*
> *Run through my veines, like to a hasty flood.*

The Master of St John's, a Welshman Owen Gwynne, had succeeded Richard Clayton the year before Herrick's entering. Clayton had superficial qualifications but an aptitude for business (he died wealthy) and the gift of shining in society. He was a popular Master but under his guidance the college not only declined academically but its numbers fell too. Matters did not improve with the later appointment, for this was

44

gained through good connexions rather than scholarship. Owen Gwynne is described as 'a soft man given altogether to ease'.

Some credit is due, however, both to Clayton and to Gwynne. During Clayton's mastership St John's built its second court, and under Gwynne its fine library was constructed and the excellent system of registration of admissions was first begun. Despite its deserved reputation for poor instruction it produced distinguished students who later ruled other colleges, Corpus Christi, St Catherine's Hall, Magdalene, Christ's and Sidney Sussex. It also produced devoted royalists : Thomas Wentworth, Archbishop Williams, and for that matter Robert Herrick.

With an inheritance of £800 he was not affluent, but compared with many undergraduates well off. He was constantly in need of money and wrote often for help to his uncle, William, who held his money and acted as banker, sending him an allowance quarterly.

He came to Cambridge without bedding, so he asked for £10 (the amount sent to him quarterly) and signed himself as 'ever to be at command and studeous to please'. He also had other individual expenses : £5 for a ten-ounce silver goblet which was part of the price of his admission as a fellow-commoner. He had to give tips to the butler and the porter, fees to the lecturer and a large sum to his tutor, bills to barbers and launderers, as well as needing money for 'sundrie occasions and chardges'.

Letters from Robert to his uncle pleading for money passed regularly from Cambridge to London. His first letter asks for £15 for his brother Thomas, whose first efforts at farming had not been successful. The money was handled through a London bookseller and the receipted letters kept by Sir William Herrick as proof that the bills were paid. In one letter Robert says that he had 'runn somewhat deepe into my Tailoures debt' . . . and later in the same letter that cares (about money) 'greatly posses me' and that consequently he was neglecting his studies. In another, during the year of his graduation, he asks his uncle to pay Arthour Johnson, bookseller in St Paul's churchyard, £10 'with as much sceleritie as you maye, though

I could wish chardges had leaden wings and Tortice feete to come vpon me . . .'

These letters are almost all addressed to Wood Street, but one is to the house in Westminster.

William, his uncle's eldest son, was at Oxford at the same time as Robert was at Cambridge. He too was living beyond his means. After two years at university the cousins planned for William to visit Cambridge to attend the festivities arranged for the gala visit of King James in 1615. William's tutor, however, asked that William should be kept at his side during the visit. It seems possible that Robert was not considered a good influence. He was doubtless one of the rowdier students at St John's and a frequent visitor to the Dolphin, the Rose, and the Mitre.

The ideal of the sober undergraduate who lived studiously in college was in actual fact the exception. Undergraduates were often drunken and lascivious. They were frequently in conflict with the townsmen and were notorious for their rudeness to strangers. Local bull and bear-pits were greatly patronized by them.

The King's gala visit was made during bad weather in March. All undergraduates were assembled by a ringing of bells to stand in respect in their hoods and gowns until the royal procession had passed. The occasion was marked by a Latin oration by Sir Francis Nethersole, the public orator, and plays were performed on four successive nights. On the first night Herrick's college, St John's, gave a play *Aemelia*.

As throughout Cambridge's history the social life of the undergraduates formed an important part in their university career. At St John's, Herrick met an influential friend in Clipsby Crew, also a fellow-commoner, who was knighted a few years after he had left the university in 1620, having matriculated fellow-commoner in 1616 and been admitted to Lincoln's Inn in 1619. (Thomas Wentworth, First Earl of Stafford (1593–1641) and John Williams, Archbishop of York (1582–1650) were also his contemporaries.) Crew was eight years younger than Robert, the son of a judge, Sir Ranulphe Crew who had an estate in Cheshire. Clipsby was a Member of Parliament from 1623–6. Evelyn states later in his diary

(1674–8) that he possessed some fine hangings and water colours by Breughel ('which I bought from him').[1]

Herrick wrote some affectionate poems to Clipsby Crew including a nuptial poem, and lines on the death of his wife Jane, aged thirty, to be carved on her tomb. He also addressed poems directly to Crew's wife; one on the death of their child.

A Nuptiall Song is a fine amalgam of conceptions based on the Jonsonian theme of Nature and Art. It is a poem of 160 lines in which such baroque couplets as:

> *The while the cloud of younglings sing,*
> *And drown yee with a flowrie Spring . . .*

are well contrasted with the fresh wholesomeness of:

> *When the bedabled Morne*
> *Washes the golden eares of corne.*

Clipsby is 'My dearest Crew'
> *That me unkindly slew* [*with love's dart*].

Later when a break came in their friendship Herrick still wrote of his devotion to Crew in a poem which concludes:

> *And rare, Ile say (my dearest* Crew*)*
> *It was full enspir'd by you.*

John Weekes, to whom Herrick dedicated three poems at various times, became a fellow of St John's College on 26 March 1613, the same year as Herrick entered. He was a close and lifelong friend. He came from Devon and it was later in

---

1. Perhaps Herrick had some of these paintings in mind when he wrote to his nephew Henry Stone (possibly 'Old Stone') *to be prosperous in his art of Painting*:

> *On, as thou hast begunne, brave youth, and get*
> *The Palme from* Urbin, Titian, Tintarret,
> Brugel *and* Coxie, *and the works out-doe*
> *Of* Holben, *and That mighty* Ruben *too.*
> *So draw, and paint, as none may do the like,*
> *No, not the glory of the World,* Vandike.

47

Devonshire that they both finally obtained livings. He was about the same age as Herrick and was obviously of an attractive temperament, cheerful, open and gifted. Weekes left Cambridge for Oxford in 1617 to take a degree in divinity.

Expenses were obviously getting out of hand – from account books preserved at Trinity Hall it appears he was still in the Hall's debt as late as 1629–30 – and studies going astray when Herrick wrote a cautious letter to his uncle asking whether he might not enter a less expensive college and study law: '. . . thus I laye open my self; that for, as much as my continuance will not long consist in the spheare where I now moue I make known my thoughts and modestly craue counsell whether it were better for me to direct my study towards the lawe or not, which yf I should (as it will not be impertinent) I can facilitie laboure my self into another colledg appointed for the like end and studyes, where I assure my self the charge will not be so great as where I now exist . . .'

No doubt this change of college was intended as a move towards a more sober life in the spirit of his poem 'His farewell to Sack'.

His next letter is addressed 'Trinitie Hall: Cam:' '. . . I haue (as I presume you know) changed my colledg, for one, where the quantitie of expence will be shortned, by reason of the priuacie of the house, where I purpose to liue recluse, till Time contract me to some other calling, striuing now with my self (retayning vpright thoughts) both sparingly to liue, thereby to shun the current of expence . . .'

He signed himself: 'Euer seruiceable to your Virtues, R. Hearick.'

Trinity Hall in Mill Street was founded by the Bishop of Norwich to train men in both civil and canon law. It was the smallest college in Cambridge and far less lavish than St John's (no tennis court or bowling green). It was obviously an easier place in which to 'live recluse' and it was a college that produced intelligent and able men.

Herrick graduated from Trinity Hall with a B.A. in 1617, and received his M.A. three years later in 1620 (the year the *Mayflower* sailed for America). Residence was not required and it is doubtful whether he spent the intervening period at Cambridge.

On 24 April 1623, together with John Weekes, Herrick stood before Thomas Dove, the Bishop of Peterborough, and was ordained deacon, and priest the following day.

The church did not demand rigid qualifications for taking the cloth and the law student was as welcome as one taking divinity. It was enough qualification if the candidate was twenty-four, had a degree and some testimonials stating that his behaviour was virtuous, and had taken the Oath of Supremacy.

Bishops could not ordain a candidate who did not already have an offering of a living and if the offer was broken the bishop was responsible for financial support until one was found. It seems likely then that some offer had been made. Obtaining a benefice was highly competitive and there was much pulling of strings.

Herrick was to be a priest of the Church of England for over half a century.

5 *Those Lyrick Feasts*

Lᴵᴛᴛʟᴇ is known about Herrick's life during the thirteen years between his graduation in 1617 and his taking up the living at Dean Prior in South Devon in September 1630. The gap in our knowledge of his life at this particular period, 'a wild unhallowed time', he called it, is unfortunate, for it was during the 1620s that he was making his name as a poet, his work for the most part circulating in manuscript form, the usual custom of the day. He was certainly a well-known literary figure when in 1625 (aged thirty-four) Richard James, a man praised by his fellow poets, and whom Jonson named the 'best of kings', printed *The Muses Dirge*. This was an elegy on the death of James I which attempts to explain why James had not received proper praise by a really famous poet:

Some Johnson, Drayton, *or some* Herrick

Herrick is thus placed in very good literary company, two distinguished and highly prized Elizabethans. This mention of his name is the first written compliment to him extant.

It is generally accepted that he spent this period of his life in London and he must have been cultivating patrons and frequenting the company of men of letters at least part of this time.

According to his own poems he mixed with several literary friends in the city taverns, in particular Ben Jonson. Apparently sometime in the 1620s he became associated with the Tribe of Ben. He was never sealed in the Tribe, but he was obviously a close friend of the dramatist. By 1623 Ben Jonson was the most influential writer in the country, with 'a vision of the glory of Rome', and a wish to bring back the Augustan Age.

The dramatist was a great drinker and talker. In the Apollo Chamber – the clubroom on the first floor of the Devil and St Dunstan at Temple Bar – he would sit on a raised seat near the bust of the Greek god himself. Herrick does not mention this tavern nor the most famous literary tavern, the Mermaid, which was in Bread Street (where Milton was born) with passage entrances from Herrick's native Cheapside and from Friday Street.[1] Curiously, nor is it mentioned by Stow in his *Survey of London*. This too was much frequented by Jonson but probably only during an earlier time, before Herrick knew him. Beaumont in his verses to Jonson wrote : 'What things we have seen done at the Mermaid.' According to tradition it was founded by Raleigh and Hakluyt was probably a patron. It was full of poets and poetasters and charged twopence more for a quart of its canary (Jonson's favourite wine and loved by Herrick too) than other taverns. It was famous for its pike.

Herrick does, however, mention other taverns frequented by the Tribe of Ben in the first verse of his ode for Jonson :

> *Ah* Ben !
> *Say how, or when*
> *Shall we thy Guests*
> *Meet at those* Lyrick *Feasts,*
> *Made at the* Sun,
> *The* Dog, *the triple* Tunne?
> *Where we such clusters had,*
> *As made us nobly wild, not mad;*
> *And yet each Verse of thine*
> *Out-did the meate, out-did the frolick wine.*

The Sun is difficult to identify, for it was a usual name for taverns. Taylor in his works I, 125, writes : 'I have found better at the three Suns in Aldersgate Street, Cripplegate and New Fish Street . . .' The Dog was the sign of a tavern possibly in Talbot Street which was afterwards known as the Sun and later still, the Queen's Arms. This place had both names at

1. Hence the different references given to it. Its tokens were inscribed 'Ye M Tavern, Cheapside'. Jonson calls it Bread Street's Mermaid and Aubrey says it was in Friday Street. A certain haberdasher describes his shop as 'over against the Mermaid tavern in Cheapside'.

different times and it may well have been the one Herrick mentions, but the situation is confusing.

The Triple Tunne or Three Tuns, the arms of the Vintner's company, were used as a tavern sign for the famous establishment of that name near the Gate in Guildhall Yard.[2]

Herrick, then, had become a literary figure. In Jonson's London, if the taverns approved a poet he had arrived. Entry was difficult but he had now achieved renown, and moreover he was pleasant, companionable and hard drinking.

His friendships and acquaintances were numerous and varied. Herrick writes of Fletcher years later as if he had known him slightly. No doubt he must have met the dramatist through his own family connexions with the Fletchers (see page 26). He also appears to have known Bishop Corbet (1582–1635), a poet and wit, who, according to Aubrey 'would sometimes take the key of the wine cellar and he and his chaplain [Dr Lushington] would go and lock themselves in to make merry'. He was the author of 'Faeries Farewell', an enthusiast for fairy lore who no doubt influenced Herrick to write in this genre.

The poet William Browne (1591–1643?), the second son of Thomas Browne, 'a gently and simple character' was also an acquaintance. He knew too John Selden the jurist (1584–1654), 'the most learned, wise and Arch-Antiquary' whom Jonson described as 'the bravest man in all languages', and Mildmay Fane (d. 1666), the second Earl of Westmorland.

An influential friend was Herrick's 'chiefe Preserver', Adrian Porter (1587–1649). He was in Buckingham's service, and groom of the bedchamber to Prince Charles. He was rewarded in May 1625 with a pension of £500, which was later converted to an annuity. Porter had been brought up in Spain and had been a page in the household of Olivares. His knowledge of Spain and Spanish brought him into diplomacy. He had Catholic sympathies and his wife was an avowed adherent to Rome. He was chiefly known for his taste in literature and painting; he bought works of art and was on friendly terms with Rubens and other painters employed by the King.

2. For reference to these taverns, see Sugden's *Topographical Dictionary to the Works of Shakespeare and his Fellow Dramatists*, 1925, and De Castro, *Dictionary of London Taverns* (Manuscript in Guildhall Library).

He was a poet himself and a patron of poets. Herrick wrote of Porter that writers would never be wanting as long as they had patrons like him : 'who . . . do'st give :'

> *Not onely subject-matter for our wit,*
> *But likewise Oyle of Maintenance to it.*

The worlds of the taverns and the court were closely knit communities. The chief poets and musicians were all courtiers of some kind, or else in famous noble households. John Suckling, George Sandys and Thomas Carew were all members of the King's Privy Council, and William Davenant was the dramatist for the King's Men Players.

Herrick is known to have been chaplain to the Duke of Buckingham, on the disastrous expedition to the Isle of Rhé (see page 55), and may well have been made a chaplain as soon as he was ordained. It is not known for certain whether he did hold any specific office at this time, but Marchette Chute[3] speculates that if a nobleman had agreed to take Herrick into his household, it would explain the speed (one day) in which he was ordained from deacon to priest.

Hazlitt[4] suggests that Herrick may have held some minor post in Westminster, perhaps in the King's Chapel at Whitehall since he had several connexions in this area including the musicians William and Henry Lawes. His acquaintance with these two brothers dates from this time.

William Lawes (1596–1662), whom Herrick calls 'the rare Musitian', was one of the musicians ordinary to Charles I, and Henry, a composer, singer and player, 'the excellent composer of his Lyrics', became Epistler in the Chapel Royal in 1626. He is best known for his music to Milton's *Comus*. Milton wrote a sonnet to him :

> *Henry, whose tuneful and well measured song*
> *First taught our English music how to span*
> *Words with just note and accent . . .*

3. *Two Gentle Men*, 1960.
4. W. Carew Hazlitt, editor of the first collection of Herrick's verse to include poems not in the original edition of 1648 and the first too to include letters (1869).

He set the Christmas songs in Herrick's *Hesperides* and his works were given court performances.

William wrote part songs and his best known vocal work is his composition to Herrick's 'To the Virgins, to make much of Time' (see page 125) which became the most popular song in seventeenth-century England. It was printed at least twenty-nine times, was a drinking song and also sung as a 'catch' which could mean that the words were distorted into puns and double meanings.

Herrick's poems were also set by Nicholas Lanier (1588–1666) the singer and composer, John Wilson (1595–1674) a Gentleman of the Chapel Royal and a singer, lutinist, and violinist who also set some of Shakespeare's verse, and Robert Ramsey (dates unknown), who was organist at Trinity College, Cambridge, from 1628–1644. (See also pages 169 and 170.)

Since Herrick had studied law at Cambridge he must too have spent some time with university friends who were now lawyers in the Inns of Court and politicians at Westminster, many of whom were poets.

Among those he came into contact with at this time, it was above all Jonson who was to have the profoundest influence. For much of this period, though, Jonson was not in good health (in 1626 and 1628 he suffered two separate strokes) and he had fallen on bad times. He was to be falsely arrested on the charge that he had eulogized the assassin of Buckingham, and he was often in acute need of money. But Jonson was at times in much favour at court and through him Herrick must have met many of the other writers of the day and men of influence. Jonson, who was of great learning and considered by his contemporaries as the greatest dramatist of his time, was not only to influence Herrick's work in such ways as his insistence that great care should be taken in reworking poems but also by introducing him to a vast inheritance (some direct) of the Humanists of the Renaissance, and of the Augustan Age and the Alexandrine poets.

This shadowy period in Herrick's life was, then, above all, the time when he gained encouragement and inspiration from Ben Jonson. This transformed him into one of the acknowledged writers of the time.

6   The Army Chaplain

ᕦᐯᕤ

Store of courage to me grant,
Now I'm turn'd a combatant:
Help me so, that I my shield
(Fighting) lose not in the field.

– from 'A Vow to Mars'

One ascertainable fact about Herrick's life at this time is in
the year 1627, when he went to the Isle of Rhé[1] as one of
the chaplains to the leader of the expedition, the Duke of
Buckingham, in aid of a Protestant Rochelle against Catholic
France.

It is not known how he obtained his commission. Some
scholars have speculated that the appointment might have
been due to the good offices of his Cambridge friend John
Weekes, who was another chaplain on the expedition,
and also a chaplain to Endymion Porter. The post might
also have been granted due to Porter's own influence. In
1625, two years before the expedition, Porter was already
a figure of some standing, held in high favour by Buckingham. Porter, then, had the power and the influence to obtain
livings.

At this time, Herrick also wisely addressed the Duke of
Buckingham (between 1623 and 1628)[2] in what nowadays
would seem abject flattery but was the accepted manner of
the time :

1. The Isle of Rhé lies just north of La Rochelle in the southern part
of the Vendée, north of Charente Maritime.
2. L. C. Martin, *The Poetical Works of Robert Herrick*, 1968.

To the High and Noble Prince, GEORGE,
Duke, Marquesse, and Earle of
Buckingham.

Never my Book's perfection did appeare,
Til I had got the name of VILLARS here.
Now 'tis so full, that when therein I look,
I see a Cloud of Glory fills my Book.
Here stand it stil to dignifie our Muse,
Your sober Hand-maid; who doth wisely chuse,
Your Name to be a Laureat Wreathe *to Hir,*
Who doth both love and feare you Honour'd *Sir.*

Buckingham, who held the rank of both admiral and general, decided to direct the war with France personally on sea and land. The expedition was to last from late June until November.

It took an inordinate time starting. In the middle of May Buckingham gave a farewell dinner at York House with a masque. On 27 June six thousand infantry and one hundred cavalry finally embarked, setting sail at four in the morning on the following Wednesday together with a special vessel with its cargo of cows, poultry and Buckingham's magnificent coach.

Before sailing Herrick wrote 'The parting Verse or charge to his supposed Wife when he travelled', in which he asks her to be chaste when he is gone. Although Edmund Gosse believed that the supposed wife was in fact the Julia of the poems and that she was Herrick's mistress during his Cambridge years, it would appear that she had in fact no more reality than the numerous other mistresses to whom he addressed his verse. Herrick was certainly not a poet of self-revelation or confession and this lady seems to be no more than a figment of his imagination.

Herrick was kept busy for there were sermons to be preached in the ships on departure to bless the journey, and others to thank God after landing. Buckingham also ordered daily camp services.

The whole expedition was dogged by bad luck and above all

by atrocious bungling. Wheat was brought but no means were provided for grinding or cooking it. The island itself offered no sustenance. It was inhabited by a few fishermen and grape growers, and its land displayed only a few shreds of vine stalks.

By early autumn Buckingham had failed to capture St Martin, the principal fort on the island, after two months' siege. The trenches dug were inadequate. It was rainy and cold. Sickness and hunger prevailed and there was talk of mutiny. Reinforcements were promised but failed to arrive. At last Buckingham, who himself displayed great personal bravery, decided to abandon the struggle and ordered his army to retreat to the ships. The line of march led across a tidal creek. A contemporary writer describes the confusion that followed. '. . . for whilest some strive to runne away, and others again hinderd them, they mutually acted the parts of enemies to each other. Thus as in troopes they labored to passe the bridge (which had no rayles or fences on eyther side) one might observe these thrustinge forward, and others puttinge them backe, untill their weapons fallinge out of their hands and grappled together, they fell arme in arme into the sea . . . In the meane while the French killed all they could overtake.'[3]

English ensigns and colours were carried away to be hung in grand display on the roof of Notre Dame while the survivors were caught in a terrible storm and some of the smaller ships were wrecked. Two-thirds of this expeditionary force never returned to England. Those combatants who did survive were unpaid and discontented. One officer who had gained distinction in the affray but had been refused promotion decided to gain revenge on the man whom he considered to be the cause of his own suffering and that of others. He stabbed and killed Buckingham at Portsmouth as he was about to embark on a second expedition to Rochelle.

There is no definite reflection of the disaster in Herrick's verse. This is not surprising, for after all he revealed very little of his personal life in his poetry. Indeed his aim was to produce lyrical, artificial verse based on classical literature, verse devoid of direct personal involvement. There are, however, lines

3. Account of Lord Herbert of Cherbury of the Expedition to the Isle of Rhé, Whittington and Wilkins, Ed. 1860.

which may be taken to show a dislike of the sea. One instance can be seen in 'His sailing from Julia'. He starts the poem with a premonition of death :

When that day comes when evening sayes I'm gone
Unto that watrie Desolation . . .

and in 'No Shipwreck of Vertue. To a friend' he tells him :

No wrack, or Bulging, thou hast cause to feare . . .

and that he will survive through virtue :

. . . all tempests to endure
And 'midst a thousand gulfs to be secure.

Rewards were given to men who had seen action as chaplains on the expedition and in 1628 Herrick was nominated to the vicarage of Dean Prior in Devonshire. His predecessor, Barnaby Potter,[4] had been promoted to the Bishopric of Carlisle on 15 March.

Herrick did not take over his parish at once as Potter, one of the King's chaplains, instead of leaving the vicarage in early spring, held Dean Prior In Commendam until Michaelmas 1630. 'In Commendam' was a device to prevent a living remaining empty until a successor could be found. In practice it was a way of collecting tithes for the bishop himself.

Herrick had to wait. At this time, in August 1629, his mother died; she had been living with her daughter Mercy Wingfield in Suffolk. Julian's will was an exact one, with bequests to her coachman and the kitchen boy. Most of the property was left to Mercy and £100 to William, her youngest child. William's wife, Robert, and Nicholas were each left a ring worth twenty shillings. Nicholas was a prosperous merchant in London, grown rich by trading with the Levant, and Robert

4. Potter, who had been educated a Puritan, had previously been presented to the vicarage of Dean Prior on 4 October 1615 by Sir Edward Giles, who had married the widow of his wife's uncle. Earlier, in October 1616, Potter had been elected provost of Queen's College, Oxford. Despite his Puritan leanings he was on good terms with the King, resulting in his appointment as Bishop.

was in holy orders, so no doubt Julian felt that the other two children were more in need of help.

In the Michaelmas of 1630 appeared :

To the Kinges most excellent Majesty
The humble peticion of Robert Hericke Chaplayne to
the late Duke of Buckingham in the Isle of Reis

Whereas yt was your Majesty's especiall fauour to bestowe on the peticioner the vicaridge of Deane, by the remoouall of Doctor Potter to the Bishopprick of Carlisle. It may now please your most sacred Majesty (the Comendation granted to him by your Majesty being expired this present Michaelmas) that your soueraigne comand may goe forth to the signature, for the dispatch of the peticioner, who shall euer pray for your Majesty's longe and happie raigne.

– caetera mando Deo.

The petitioner was dispatched.

7 To lothèd Devonshire

To set out from London to South Devon was no small undertaking. Roads were in a worse condition than they had been in Roman times, and as communications were very bad Herrick must have felt he was virtually leaving civilization for exile. The concept of distance was very different from what we have nowadays, the highest speed being the pace of a horse, and his goal must have seemed very distant. As there was no immediate communication, ties with London were virtually nil during a long journey. Near London the roads were covered with gravel, but they would sink into a sea of mud when drenched in rain, making them difficult to negotiate. Further out of London the highways were often abominable. In some areas enclosures made the ways so narrow that a coach or a wagon could not pass through, and pack horses had to be used instead. But though by modern standards the roads were poor, there was already in the 1630s an extensive regular network of carriers linking London with the provincial towns and regular coaches had started to run along some of the main routes.

It was not until the middle of the seventeenth-century that coaches with glass windows were introduced into England. Even then, gentlemen preferred to make their journeys on horseback and it was in this way that he most likely travelled. It was easy to hire horses and English inns generally had excellent arrangements for relays of post horses. Possibly he went from London to Plymouth or Exeter, then open to sea traffic, by boat. But one can gather from his verse that he was not a good sailor and would have preferred land travel.

We can visualize the journey with some clarity, for the climate was roughly the same : the same winds, unpredictable showers and sudden sunlight. The hills, valleys and plains were similar to what they are today, but there was one aspect which the present day traveller would soon notice. Everything he passed except the country mansions was on a small scale —the houses, the rooms, even the men themselves. One outstanding difference in the country scene he would see would be that the ploughing was carried out by oxen. Being autumn the roads were probably in a bad state, through rain, particularly in the west.

People rode their own horses or hired them at two shillings the first day and one shilling and sixpence thereafter. They either had to ride the animals back to their place of hire or arrange for their return. The fodder had to be provided out of the rider's own pocket.

Covered wagons which took both passengers and goods from city to city were used only by the poor, although they were sometimes patronized by foreign visitors. Most travellers rode together, often armed with daggers and pistols. They did so for greater protection against robbers and also for company on the long journey. They avoided travelling by night and looked for an inn before dark for fear of highwaymen.

Some of the inns were good. A meal could cost as much as four shillings and sixpence. One could book a meal in a private room and musicians were available for entertainment. A traveller could also eat cheaply at the public table.

Other inns were infected with vermin and insects. Fleas were not uncommon. As in London taverns, there was a great deal of smoking. The habit was considered health giving.

Thirty miles a day was a good average for a traveller on horseback. It probably took Herrick five days to make his journey. At the end, when he arrived at the village, he must have been somewhat dismayed by its isolation. On his arrival too it is unlikely that he found any spontaneous welcome. Dr Barnabus Potter was popular with his parishioners because of his tendencies towards Puritanism. Herrick was a Cavalier, a Royalist with no Puritan inclinations, and moreover, he was a Londoner, a 'foreigner'.

According to the episcopal register he was installed as Vicar of Dean Prior on 29 October 1630.

8 Rurall Privacie

The countryside around Dean Prior[1] (pl. 26) is composed of large rolling hills, beech trees, coppices and deep-cut, stoney Devon lanes. The soil below the village of Dean and at Dean Prior is brown and not the red earth found in many other parts of the county.

The church and adjoining vicarage with its outhouses (pl. 20–22) set in a valley are now situated on one steep side of a busy dual carriageway, part of the route from Exeter to Plymouth.

The peace of the beautifully kept vicarage garden is perpetually disturbed by the noise of traffic, though somewhat curiously within the vicarage and the church itself complete silence remains.

The old road leading from Buckfastleigh and Dean towards South Brent still exists on the hill flanking the other side of the valley.

The present vicarage dates mostly from the eighteenth-century, but the structure still enfolds sections and objects from the building as it was during Herrick's tenure. There remain a few latticed windows with the original catches, the ceilings and doorways show where they have been raised and Herrick's

1. *Denu* is the Old English word for valley. *Dean Prior* was known as *Dena* in 1086 and had become *La Dene* in 1244, *Dene Priores* in 1316 and *Dene Pryour* by 1415. The manor was held from the eleventh century by the priors of Plympton Priory, hence the second part of the place's name. The part around the church was known as *Over Dean* and *Nether Dean* (O.E. *neðera*, nether, lower) was used for the place now simply called *Dean*, further along the road to Ashburton.

The stream Dean Bourne flows under the road just before one reaches the village of Dean from Dean Prior. It is joined to the River Dart. Earlier it was known as Deneburne (O.E. *Denn*, valley; *burna*, stream, burn). The local people still pronounce *Bourne* as *burn* (see pl. 23).

kitchen, where his housekeeper Prudence Baldwin used to cook for him, appears to keep its original shape. Under the roof, part of the supporting structure retains sections that used to carry the original thatch, Herrick's 'humble Roof' which was 'weather-proof'.

Most interesting of all, in its original condition, stands the wine cellar, built of the local stone. One enters down a step made of Ashburton marble and a torch shows that Herrick's wooden wine bins still stand intact.

The large steeply-sloping lawn in the vicarage garden (pl. 20) sprouts snowdrops in late winter and, in spring time, daffodils.

This lawn leads upwards to a pathway running parallel to the vicarage lined with beech trees about a hundred years old. This path is known locally as 'Herrick's walk' (pl. 24), but there is no evidence to show whether Herrick ever did use this path, though it might well have existed, with or without trees on either side, when he lived at the vicarage.

The outhouses, made of local stone, and a kitchen garden, both from Herrick's time, still exist. No doubt it was in one of these buildings (pl. 22) that he kept some of the pets he mentions in his verse.

In the churchyard, his grave has long remained unmarked. Recently a stone has been erected over a supposed resting place. Earlier this century a sexton by mistake dug up bones covered in leather clothing with silver buckles in this spot. It is located in front of what used to be the main entrance to the church which has long been walled up.

The church itself (pl. 21), much restored, has a nave and two aisles divided by low octagonal granite piers. The font, which is Norman (pl. 25), is circular and made of red sandstone. There is a chalice and cover by Jons of Exeter, dated 1576.

On one wall there is a monument to Sir Edward Giles (d. 1642) and his family with the epitaph by Herrick carved underneath it.

A tablet to Herrick was set up in 1857 and there is another one to Herrick's maid Prudence Baldwin, also of a late date. A small case displays a few of the books devoted to the poet and editions of his works.

In the 1630s, Devon, as now, was good farming country, producing mutton, wool and cider. Oliver Cromwell said it was the best agricultural county in England. Devon had been in a state of decay a century earlier, but an Act was passed in 1540 to encourage house building.

The South Devon area was a district of good farming and of small wastes and commons, and had, and still has a milder and more healthy climate than any other part of England, but the south-easterly winds could ruin the corn and blow the fruit off the trees. The apple trees were small and cider-producing.

Near the larger towns there was an ample supply of fish which, added to the ordinary diet, made the mass of the inhabitants healthy, vigorous and long-living. The cattle were largely of the same breed as those in the north of the country; the sheep the dim-faced not sheep. Sheep stealing was, as ever, prevalent on Dartmoor. Mules and asses were much used for carrying. The small town of Kingsbridge nearby produced its white ale, brewed in malt with eggs, flour, salt and a mysterious ingredient called grout. It was very potent. In Totnes a well-known serge was made by the local women.

Herrick's parish covered some four thousand acres. It was made up of three villages: Dean Prior, Dean Combe and Dean Church. Dean Prior was the largest. His church and small vicarage, which he called 'his cell', lay separate from the houses.

A village community at this time was a very closely knit one, and life was centred around the church. Each villager was well-known to his neighbour and each criticized the other publicly. Herrick did not take to them. The people in his parish, as in most other parts of rural England, were primitive. They did not change their clothes often and lived for the most part in hovels. In 'To Dean-bourn, a rude River in Devon, by which sometimes he lived', Herrick called them

> *A people currish; churlish as the seas;*
> *And rude (almost) as rudest Salvages.*

and in 'To his Household gods' he wrote of the general primitiveness of life in Devon:

> *. . . First let us dwell on rudest seas;*
> *Next, with severest salvages;*

Tempora cinxisset Foliorum densior umbra :
Debetur Genio laurea Sylva tuo.
Tempora et Illa Tibi mollis redimisset Oliva;
Scilicet excludis Versibus Arma tuis.
Admisces Antiqua Novis, Iucunda Severis :
Hinc Iuvenis discat, Foemina,Virgo, Senex.
Ut solo minor es Phoebo, sic major es Unus
Omnibus, Ingenio, Mente, Lepore, Stylo .
W. Marshall Fecit·   scripsit I.H.C. W. M.

1   *Robert Herrick as he appeared in 1648 on the title-page of*
Hesperides

2 *Herrick's godfather and uncle, Robert Herrick*

3 *Sir William Herrick, Robert's uncle to whom he was apprenticed as a goldsmith*

4 *Mary Bond, Herrick's paternal grandmother, at the age of ninety*

5 *Cornelius Dankerts' map, made about 1645*

6 A prospect of London and the Thames from above Greenwich. Almost certainly painted by a Flemish painter between 1620 and 1630, this is believed to be the earliest painted view of London seen from a distance

7 Engraving by Wenceslaus Hollar, about 1666

A TRVE AND EXACT PROSPECT OF THE FAMOVS CITY OF LONDON FROM S. MARIE OVERS STEEPLE IN SOUTHWARKE IN ITS FLOURISHING CONDITION BEFORE THE FIRE

LONDON

THE RIVER THAMES

ANOTHER PROSPECT OF THE SAYD CITY TAKEN FROM THE SAME PLACE AS IT APPEARETH NOW AFTER THE SAD CALAMITIE AND DESTRVCTION BY FIRE. In the Yeare M.DC.LXVI

8 Cheapside and Cheapside Cross in 1638, on the occasion of Marie de Medici's visit to Charles and Henrietta Maria

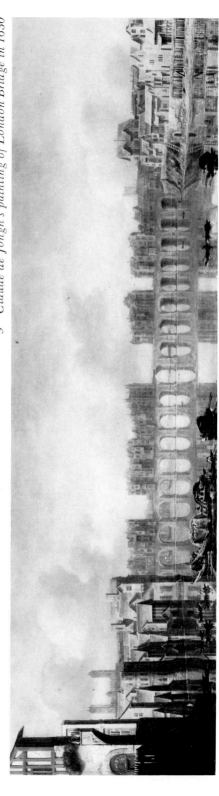

9 Claude de Jongh's painting of London Bridge in 1630

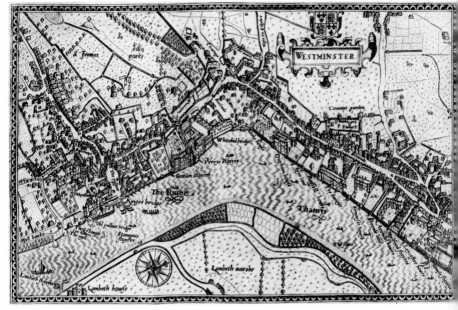

10   Norden's map of Westminster in 1593

11   Section of Aga's plan of Elizabethan London

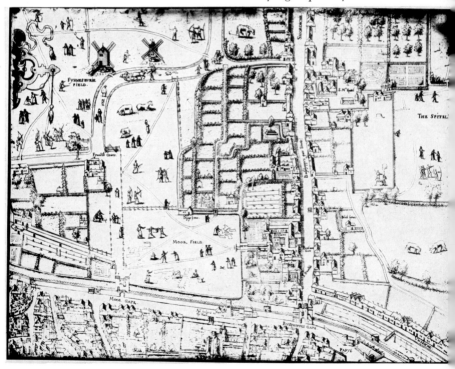

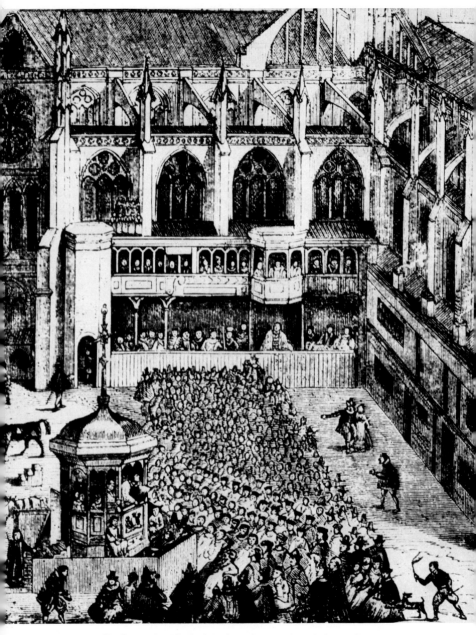

12 *St Paul's Cross in 1616 showing the open pulpit at the N.E. of the Cathedral*

13 Cambridge from the east and west sides engraved by David Loggan in 1690

Last, let us make our last abode,
Where humane foot, as yet, n'er trod:
Search worlds of Ice; and rather there
Dwell, then in lothèd Devonshire.

In an age when classes mixed freely and when Herrick himself could be coarse if he so wished there yet existed an un-
bridgeable distance between this parson and his flock. His
reaction was not unlike that of another poet and clergyman,
George Crabbe, who a century and a half later wrote in 'The
Village' (1783) about the native population of Suffolk :

Here joyless roam a wild amphibious race,
With sullen wo display'd in every face;
Who, far from civil arts and social fly,
And scowl at strangers with suspicious eye.

This was far from his ideal of country life as Herrick expounded
it earlier, to his brother Thomas (*c* 1610), saying he was 'Thrice
and above, blest', since :

Could'st leave the City, for exchange, to see
The Countries sweet simplicity . . .

He was instead confronted with peasants like the shoresmen
mentioned a few lines later in 'The Village' who produced in
Crabbe a very similar kind of disillusion :

I sought the simple life that Nature yields;
Rapine and Wrong and Fear usurp'd her place
And a bold, artful, surly savage race;
Who, only skill'd to take the finny tribe,
The yearly dinner, or septennial bribe . . .

Before Herrick arrived in Dean Prior an attempt had been
made to suppress wakes. They were considered degrading,
rowdy and encouraged extreme drunkenness. This was part of
a concerted attempt by the Puritans to suppress the sensual
and erect strict doctrines of abstinence and hard work. But the
old customs were deeply implanted and Herrick speaks of the
country people in his poem on wakes as :

Drench't in Ale, or drown'd in Beere . . .

They were without question Breughelesque.

The names of the subjects of Herrick's epigrams, Scobble, Madge, Dundridge, Coone and others appear in the Dean Prior register. Not one appears in a flattering light in his verse. Coone 'so dully smells'. Madge goes to the postern every morning 'his teeth all out' to rinse and wash his gums and Scobble whips his wife for 'whoredom'. Other names are perhaps disguised but no doubt the portraits are drawn from reality as Skoles who 'stinks so deadly' that his breeches are 'unwilling to clothe his dampish buttocks' or Jone who has only seven hairs, three black and four white. They could have been very little different from the Devon peasantry described about two centuries later by Mrs A. E. Bray in 1838 in *Traditions, Legends, Superstitions and Sketches of Devonshire* as 'not overclean' and wearing patched clothes, with hair bleached by the sun. She writes that the peasantry saluted strangers with a bob of the head and their cheeks could hardly be compared with roses, but were rather red 'as a piece of beef'. They were brutish. In an official survey by Charles Vancouver produced in 1808, the Devonians are said to have treated their horses worse than 'anywhere in Britain except Ireland'.

He found himself, then, living in a place far removed in his mind from a country idyll, in a landscape very different from the cultivated fields and slopes of Middlesex and Surrey, totally unrelated to his own carefully contrived Arcadia. As the Reverend J. Whitfield wrote of Herrick in his *Rambles in Devonshire*, 1854 : 'He set no store on Nature, unless embellished in the trim alleys and improved in the parterres, of Whitehall.'

It could not have been long before he was homesick not only for London but for his youth and bygone Elizabethans, and for the social and literary life of the capital. It is easy to imagine, when the news of Jonson's death in 1637 eventually came through to Dean Prior, how isolated and lonely he must have felt.

In that remote part of Devon, the local speech, more dialectal than now, retaining some words of Celtic origin, must have seemed alien to him. There was a large gulf separating him from his surroundings. He must have found it very difficult to show Christian sympathy and administer to his parishioners.

He was at first, and often later, lonely with the identical 'enforced solitarinesse' that still another famous parson living in rural seclusion, Robert Burton, has expressed. It is a solitariness which : '. . . produceth his effect soonest in such as have spent their time jovially, peradventure in all honest recreations, in good company, in some great family or populous City, and are upon a sudden confined to a desart countrey Cottage farre off, restrained of their liberty, and barred from their ordinary associates; solitarinesse is very irkesome to such, most tedious . . .'

In a poem 'To Sir Clipsebie Crew' Herrick complains :

> *Since to th'Countrey first I came,*
> *I have lost my former flame:*
> *And, methinks, I not inherit,*
> *As I did, my ravisht spirit.*
> *If I write a Verse, or two,*
> *'Tis with very much ado . . .*

The winter evenings must have seemed long and dark with tedium. He had of course his books – no doubt some of the classics, the Bible and such works as were on most literate people's bookshelves as Foxe's *The Book of Martyrs* and almost certainly, as will be seen later, Burton's *The Anatomy of Melancholy*. It was completely peaceful, no doubt, but he must have longed for the activity of London streets and the noise of the taverns. Above all he must have lacked conversation. In London entertainment and friends were all within easy compass. At Dean Prior he had a fair walk to the nearest neighbours with whom he would have anything in common, and Exeter was a long horseride away.

No doubt his disillusionment and discontent must have led his thoughts to compare his lot with the banishment of Ovid from Rome to the half barbaric town of Tomi near the mouth of the Danube.

His loneliness was broken by the arrival of his sister-in-law Elizabeth Herrick (very probably the wife of William, but possibly the wife of Thomas) who came to keep house for him until 1643 when she died and was buried at Dean Prior. He wrote her two poems : 'No Spouse but a Sister'

Which I will keep embrac'd
And kisse, but yet be chaste.

and an epitaph

Next, how I love thee, that my griefe must tell
Wherein thou liv'st for ever. Deare farewell.

Little by little he began to find some contentment in his retreat and saw the customs of May Day, harvest time and Twelfth Night as part of an ageless culture. There were connexions, though rather slight, between this Anglo-Saxon Arcadia and his classical world. There were scenes to watch and customs to enjoy : the yule-log at Christmas and May dancing. In the cider districts there was the wassailing of the apple trees. Herrick wrote 'The Wassaile' and made other references to the custom in his verses.

Wassailing consisted in drinking a health to one of the apple trees, with the wish that it should bear much fruit. This wish was mostly fulfilled as the best tree in the orchard was invariably toasted, 'Health to thee, good apple-tree'. Roasted apples or toast was added to the cider itself. When everyone had drunk, the remainder of the bowl's contents was sprinkled on the apple-tree. This custom seems to be a relic of the sacrifice of the Ancients to Pomona. Its similarity to the customs of the Ancients can hardly have escaped Herrick.

Another custom prevalent at that time was for all the inhabitants of a village to gather to reap the farmer's wheat. This was done of a free will and without pay and was followed by a great deal of drinking, noise and merrymaking.

During Rogation Week there was a ceremony in which Herrick must have participated. Then it was the clergyman's duty to lead his congregation round the bounds of the parish as a reminder of the landmarks. The parish had no legal boundary, only a traditional one that remained in the memories of the parishioners. It was also the annual duty of the parson

to bless the young crops, repeating the Mosaic formula:
'Cursed be he that removeth his neighbour's landmark.'

Herrick too had to help manage and police the parish with
the churchwardens to see that the alms chest in the church was
kept well locked, and to make sure that another chest which
contained the parish register and records of all weddings,
baptisms and burials was kept safely from unwanted intruders.

The church was the focus of parish life and the parson
represented its authority. He was the centre of his small community.

Herrick's income, though sufficient, was certainly not large.
It was fixed in a period of inflation. He received a maximum
of thirty pounds a year. His expenses, however, were small and
he also received some extra fees. One shilling for a peal of bells
at a wedding, two shillings and eight pence for a burial if the
coffin were included and two pence for Easter offerings at
communion. Some of the fees went to the parish fund, some
to the clerk, some to the sexton but some to the parson himself.
Herrick also had the right to give dispensations to his
parishioners to allow them to eat meat during Lent at the
standard rate of six shillings and eight pence.

A larger part of the parson's income came in tithes, a tenth
part of the land's increase. This offering, paid twice a year,
was once voluntary but in Herrick's time it was a compulsory
payment. As he was a vicar and not a rector Herrick did not
receive all the tithes in Dean Prior. Moreover, they were not
easy to collect from the farmers, for tithes from vegetables,
lambs and eggs were virtually impossible to assess accurately.

Herrick appeared to take the whole matter with equanimity.
He writes in 'The Tythe. To the Bride':

> *If nine times you your Bride-groome kisse;*
> *The tenth you know the Parsons is.*
> *Pay then your Tythe; and doing thus,*
> *Prove in your Bride-bed numerous . . .*

Although he had not yet come to terms with his surroundings
Herrick began to write verse in Dean Prior which proved to be
a subtle combination of classical themes and concepts blended
with a particular wholesomeness and freshness taken from the

English countryside. Isolated, he had to seek pleasure and happiness for the greater part in his imagination, in poetry. He reveals in his 'Discontents in Devon' :

More discontents I never had
Since I was born, then here;
Where I have been, and still am sad,
In this dull Devon-shire*:*
Yet justly too I must confesse;
I ne'r invented such
Ennobled numbers for the Presse,
Then where I loath'd so much.

By 'ennobled' numbers he does not mean specifically Christian poems only, but in fact his best verse of all categories.

L. C. Martin in his introduction to the Oxford edition of *The Poetical Works of Robert Herrick* (1968 edition) says there is reason to believe that some of his best poems were, in fact, written in Devonshire in the 1630s :

. . . there is some connexion, however tenuous and broken, between the order of the poems as they were printed in *Hesperides* and the order in which they were written can be supported by evidence that some of the influences on Herrick's poetry appear to be more pronounced in the earlier or later part of the secular volume. Thus the influence of Horace and Ovid is more noticeable in the first half, and of Martial and Tacitus in the second. That of Burton, unavailable before 1621, when the *Anatomy* was first published, cannot be very surely illustrated from any poems which are datable up to 1631 by their occasions or circumstances, and from few of the poems found in manuscripts. The influence is at least arguably at work in some of the best-known pieces, 'Delight in Disorder', 'Corinna's going a Maying' (final stanza especially), and 'Bid me to live'. It pervades *Hesperides* but is more frequently observable in the second half than in the first. The third and fourth editions of the *Anatomy* appeared in 1628 and 1632.

We learn much of his life in his vicarage from his verse when, in the end, he had come to terms with his new surroundings. He reflects a calm contentment when writing about his house, his maid and his pet animals. In 'To his ever-loving God' in *His Noble Numbers* appear these clear-cut lines :

> *I kenn my home; and it affords some ease,*
> *To see far off the smoking villages.*

In 'A Thanksgiving to God, for his House' he writes that he lives dry in his 'cell' under a weatherproof roof. His threshold is worn by the poor to whom he gives advice and food. His parlour hall and kitchen are small. A little buttery contains a bin with a loaf of bread untouched by mice. His fire is made of brittle sticks of thorn and briar. There he sits glowing contentedly in its heat. His hearth glitters with 'guiltlesse mirth'.

He enjoys his Worts, Purslain and the Messe of Water-cresse and his 'beloved' beetroot.

He has a wassail bowl filled to the brink and spiced. He says God sees to it that his hen lays him an egg each day. He also has healthy ewes who bear him twins yearly, and

> *. . . the conduits of my Kine*
> *Run Creame, (for Wine.)*
> *All these, and better Thou dost send*
> *Me, to this end,*
> *That I should render, for my part,*
> *A thankfull heart; . . .*

In 'His Grange, or private wealth' he enumerates his housekeeper, Prudence Baldwin, and a list of animals including his spaniel Tracie on whom he wrote an epitaph which is simple and touching :

> *Now thou art dead, no eye shall ever see,*
> *For shape and service,* Spaniell *like to thee.*
> *This shall my love doe, give thy sad death one*
> *Teare, that deserves of me a million.*

He also kept a pet sparrow *Phill* on which, when it died, he too wrote an elegy.

In 'His Grange or private wealth', Herrick reveals himself very much the Englishman :

> *Though Clock,*
> *To tell how night drawes hence, I've none,*
> *A Cock,*
> *I have, to sing how day drawes on.*
> *I have*
> *A maid* (my Prew) *by good luck sent,*
> *To save*
> *That little, Fates me gave or lent.*
> *A Hen*
> *I keep, which creeking day by day,*
> *Tells when*
> *She goes her long white egg to lay.*
> *A goose*
> *I have, which, with a jealous eare,*
> *Lets loose*
> *Her tongue, to tell what danger's neare.*
> *A Lamb*
> *I keep (tame) with my morsells fed,*
> *Whose Dam*
> *An Orphan left him (lately dead.)*
> *A Cat*
> *I keep, that playes about my House,*
> *Grown fat,*
> *With eating many a miching Mouse.*
> *To these*
> *A *Trasy I do keep, whereby   *His Spaniel*
> *I please*
> *The more my rurall privacie:*
> *Which are*
> *But toyes, to give my heart some ease:*
> *Where care*
> *None is, slight things do lightly please.*

In 'His content in the Country' Herrick says that he is living frugally :

> *Though ne'r so mean the Viands be,*
> *They well content my* Prew *and me*

He again writes he is content with the vegetables mentioned earlier, wort, beet and also pea and bean.

He has to pay no rent for his 'poore Tenement'. He and Prue do not have to fear any usurer or landlord and 'our Peaceful slumbers' are not disturbed by the Quarter-day. He adds that 'we eate our own' and are not dependent on others. He concludes:

> *We blesse our Fortunes, when we see*
> *Our own beloved privacie:*
> *And like our living, where w'are known*
> *To very few, or else to none.*

Of his maid Prue's devotion to him he writes:

> *These* Summer-Birds *did with thy Master stay*[2]
> *The times of warmth; but then they flew away;*
> *Leaving their Poet (being now grown old)*
> *Expos'd to all the coming Winters cold.*
> *But thou* kind Prew *did'st with my Fates abide,*
> *As well the Winters, as the Summers Tide:*
> *For which thy Love, live with thy Master here,*
> *Not two, but all the seasons of the yeare.*

He records on one occasion that

> *Prue, my dearest maid, is sick*
> *Almost to be Lunatick*

and concludes in a classical vein which today would appear to lack depth of feeling but for him would only appear genuine:

> *Aesculapius!*[3] *come and bring*
> *Means for her recovering;*
> *And a galant Cock shall be*
> *Offer'd up by Her, to Thee.*

Prudence outlived Herrick by four years. She was buried at Dean Prior on 6 January 1678. Earlier Herrick wrote this epitaph 'Upon Prew his Maid':

2. Possibly referring to summer visitors.
3. A god of healing, incarnated on earth as a snake.

In this little Urne is laid
Prewdence Baldwin (once my maid)
From whose happy spark here let
Spring the purple Violet.

*   *

Herrick's solitude was, however, not quite as absolute as his poems suggest. According to Wood he 'became much beloved by the gentry of those parts' – the Giles family, the Northleighs, Lowmans and Yards.

The Stuart squirearchy lived by no means an isolated bucolic life. They formed part of a movement in an active society. There was some difference in sophistication between those living in the west and those resident near London, but it was only a relative difference. Herrick, though, who was used to the company of Ben Jonson, and other writers, musicians and those near to the Court, must have found limitations in their conversation. Though there was contact with London, the capital was distant and their attitudes and latest knowledge of events was naturally often secondhand.

His verse must have circulated among the local gentry but their appreciation and criticism was a far cry from the approval or condemnation of his fellow writers.

Devonshire was pre-eminently a county of country gentlemen during this period.[4] There were few noblemen and few great landowners. This gentry was influential both socially and politically, not the least the families of Herrick's district.

Sir Edward Giles, a baronet knighted by James I at his coronation, lived throughout the year at the manor at Dean Court (the house still exists though changed since Herrick's day). He had moved his household to Dean Prior from the family seat at Bowden near Totnes, his birthplace. (The manor of

---

4. Forest clearance in Devonshire was at its height during the period 1205–1349. Freehold estates developed, thus producing a new class of minor freeholders who were the ancestors of the lesser squires of the sixteenth, seventeenth, and eighteenth centuries. The Dean Prior area became owned by a number of old freehold families as the frontiers of cultivation were pushed farther north towards the Moor. These died out in Elizabethan times and the estates were taken over by others.

Dean Prior had been bought at the Dissolution from Henry
VIII by William Giles.)

Since he was childless, Sir Edward Giles made a relative
his heir to his original property, to live there and run the place.
He was about fifty when Herrick knew him and was living a
life of retirement from parliamentary duties, having represented
Totnes in the Commons during the reigns of James I and
Charles I. He had been Sheriff of the County in 1613 and
earlier a soldier serving Elizabeth in the Low Countries.

Giles must have been glad at the arrival of the new vicar
fresh from London, and Herrick in turn pleased with the com-
panionship and hospitality of the local squire and his wife
Mary. Dean Court stood in a walled park about half a mile
from the vicarage. Their friendship was only of seven years
duration as Sir Edward Giles died at Christmas 1637 and was
buried in Herrick's parish church on 28 December. Mary Giles
lived on at Dean Prior until her death five years later.

The house went to the relations of Sir Edward, whom he
had made his heirs, the Yard family. Edward Yard, Giles's
great-nephew, took up residence at Dean Court. Herrick baptized in 1637, 1638 and 1639 Edward's sons Giles, Edward
and Sampson.

Edward Yard also had a sister a year younger than himself,
Lettice, whom Herrick called 'the most witty Mrs Lettice
Yard' in his occasional verses on her marriage to Henry North-
leigh. The Northleighs settled in Dean Prior and their children's
names are recorded in the parish register.

Lettice and Edward had two half sisters, Amy and Grace,
the daughters of Herrick's predecessor as vicar who had married
Lettice's mother Elizabeth after she had been three years a
widow. Grace was pretty. Herrick writes of her 'comely face'
whose :

> ... *every portion else,*
> *Keepes line for line Beauties Parallels.*

To Amy he made an even more amorous approach :
> To Mistress *Amie Potter*

> *Ai me! I love, give him your hand to kisse*
> *Who both your wooer, and your Poet is.*

Nature has pre-compos'd us both to Love;
Your part's to grant; my Scean must be to move.
Deare, can you like, and liking love your Poet?
If you say (I) Blush-guiltinesse will shew it.
Mine eyes must wooe you; (though I sigh the while)
True Love is tonguelesse as a Crocodile.
And you may find in Love these differing Parts;
Wooers have Tongues of Ice, but burning hearts.

Herrick did not confine his love poems, whether of imagined love or genuine, to the Yard family alone. He also wrote 'The Meddow verse or Aniversary to Mistris Bridget Lowman', a niece of Sir Edward Giles, asking her to be the 'medows Deity'.

He was not then living the life of a hermit; nor was his isolation from other areas of Devon complete, though doubtless weeks and months of solitude must have weighed upon him. The high road linked his village with Exeter about twenty miles to the north and he must have travelled along it to the county town. It was then known as Little London. Well known for its cloths and serge, it was a busy port with numerous markets and shops, and walks and bowling greens in the suburbs. As it was the ecclesiastical centre of Devon, Herrick inevitably visited there on occasion. The bishop, Joseph Hall, was literary and learned and came from Leicestershire like Herrick's family. He had been Bishop of Exeter three years before Herrick's arrival at Dean Prior. His palace was not in full use, being partly employed as a warehouse, as revenues had declined since the Middle Ages. The cathedral itself was famous for its organ and it would seem likely that Herrick, who had a love of music, must have heard the instrument played.

In the cathedral close good ale was served and the local divines were, like Herrick, convivial drinkers. Some of the names of the clergy 'High Sons of Pith', mentioned in the manuscript of his poem 'His Age', were clergymen settled in the West Country. Martin Nansogg, who graduated from Trinity Hall in 1613, came from a long line of local vicars. He was nominated to the archdeanery of Cornwall, but Bishop Hall found him unsatisfactory as a chaplain, so he was never installed. He later became Vicar of Cornwood, north-east of Plymouth near Ivybridge, in 1628. James Smith, listed in the same poem, was another local divine and a poet. He had served on the expedition to the Isle of Rhé, as chaplain to Henry Rich, Earl of Holland, when Rich was commanding a fleet with reinforcements to Buckingham. In 1639 he became Rector of King's Nympton near South Molton in north Devon and later precentor and canon at Exeter. He was a writer of light verse and collaborated with Sir John Minnes (Mynts), appointed commander of the King's navy, in editing *Witt's Recreations* and other works which included their own and Herrick's poems. In *Musarum Deliciae* there is mention of Herrick in 'To Dr Wicks an invitation to London':

> *... and that old Sack,*
> *Young Herrick took to entertain*
> *The muses in a sprightly vein,*
> *A London goal with friends and drink*
> *Is worth your vicarage, I think.*

Their collections sold well, as they included bawdy passages.

John Weekes (see pp. 47, 49), described by Wood[5] as 'a jocular person' and whose 'unlicensed jocularity was so distasteful to the King' and to whom 'His Age' is dedicated, turns up again in Herrick's life. He became Rector of Shirwell (near Barnstaple) in Devon in 1627; he had the prebendary of Bristol in 1633 and was installed as Vicar of Banwell in Somerset in 1640. He also became Dean of St Burion in Cornwall and Chaplain to Archbishop Laud. Between 1629 and 1634 he tried to persuade Endymion Porter to 'be mentioned to the King for Diptford' (at the time when Herrick's living became vacant). He would have been only four-and-a-half miles south of Dean Prior. Porter, however, could be of no help.

Weekes was a widower when Herrick first came to Devon, his wife Bridget (the daughter of Sir Richard Grenville of the *Revenge*) having died in 1627, a few months before setting out on the expedition to the Isle of Rhé. In 1636 he married Grace Cary, the sister of the Dean of Exeter. The marriage

5. *Fasti*, ed. Bliss ii, vol. 68.

took place in Exeter Cathedral. It is attractive to speculate that Herrick was present.

Apart from clerical companions Herrick also had contact with friends in the law. Sir George Parry, the Recorder of Exeter (of the Inner Temple), John Were, 'his honoured friend' (also of the Inner Temple), an Exeter alderman, and his 'peculiar friend' Sir Thomas Shapcot who lived in the parish of Knowstone but spent most of his time in Exeter. Herrick valued Shapcot because he prized 'things that are curious and un-familiar' and he dedicated his 'Oberon's Feast' and 'Oberon's Palace' to him. These were all Royalists and Herrick's sympathies also kept him in contact with another lawyer, John Merrifield, Sir Thomas Heale, M.P. for Plymouth, one of the Royalist commanders, and Sir John Berkeley, the Governor of Exeter who captured the city in September 1643 and held it to September 1646.

Such contacts must have been a solace for Herrick in his solitude, but for a Londoner sequestered in the depths of the country they must have seemed too tenuous.

On one hand he appears to have found contentment and peace at Dean Prior, on the other an isolation and boredom bred of a deprivation of chosen company.

9 Noe Lycence for non-residence

⟨∿∾⟩

The first of Herrick's acknowledged poems to be published appeared in the revised edition of Stow's *Survey of London*. In a discussion of the monuments in St Margaret's Church, Westminster, epitaphs are quoted. Amongst these was Herrick's memorial to his niece, 'Upon his Kinswoman Mistris Elizabeth Herrick'.

A little later an early draft poem of 'Oberon's Feast' was published, also anonymously, in a collection of five poems on fairyland. His poems are to be found in other collections: in 1660 in *An Addition of some Excellent Poems, to those precedent, of Renowned Shakespeare, By other Gentlemen*. Other contributors to this collection included Jonson and Beaumont.

Apart from these collections his poems had only circulated in manuscript form – one of his poems is known to have twenty-four copies – and they were known to many and were recited even 138 years after his death (see pp. 97 and 98).

Although Herrick wrote for a restricted public – gentlemen versed in the classics – some of his verse, like that of other poets, was known by the ordinary people. One is reminded of the milkmaid in Izaak Walton's *The Compleat Angler* who sang to Picator and Venator Marlowe's 'Come live with me and be my love' and also Raleigh's reply.

In towns perhaps half the population could read. In the countryside the proportion was much smaller. But the oral tradition was strong and it represented the common consciousness not only of poetry but also the history of the past. Herrick's poems were repeated from mouth to mouth.

An entry in the Stationers' Register on 29 April 1640 shows an application by Andrew Crooke, who kept a bookshop in St Paul's Churchyard, under the sign of The Green Dragon,

79

to publish 'The severall Poems written by Master Robert Herrick'. No such volume is extant, and it seems that Herrick had to wait another eight years before seeing his work in print.

It would have been impossible to arrange the printing of this book from Devonshire and he would have had to go to London.

He was in fact in London around this time, for an undated private note was issued by William Dell, the secretary of Archbishop Laud, a man active in detecting and punishing, on behalf of his master, the misdeeds of corrupt clergymen:

> Thomsin Parsons hath had a bastard lately: shee was brought to bed at Greenwich.
>
> Mr Henrique a minister possest of a very good living in Devonshire hath not resided there having noe Lycence for his non-residence and not being chapline to any nobleman or man qualified by law I heare his lodging is at Westminster in the Little Amrie at Nicholas Wilkes his house where the said Thomsin Parsons lives.

The paper is endorsed 'Mr Delles man abt. Mr Henrique a minister'.

According to ecclesiastical law, Herrick, as a vicar, could not leave his parish unless he had dispensation from his bishop and it would appear he was in London without leave of absence. The charge was not brought and there is no record of corroboration of this report. The investigation was the function of the local diocese and the information should have been sent to Bishop Hall in Exeter. No record has so far been found. The allegation could well be true, however, but Laud was far too busy during this time of national crisis to look into the alleged misdeeds of an obscure vicar from Devonshire.

Tomasin, aged twenty-two at this date, was the daughter of John Parsons who had died seventeen years earlier and was survived by his wife, Jane, and their three children, the other two being William and Dorothy. He was a composer and organist of St Margaret's, Westminster, and in 1621 was appointed organist and master of choristers at Westminster Abbey where he was later buried in the cloisters.

Tomasin was christened in 1616 and was twenty-seven years younger than Herrick.

He wrote her a two line poem :

> *Grow up in Beauty, as thou do'st begin*
> *And be of all admired*, Tomasin.

and also a four line poem to her elder sister Dorothy :

> *If you aske me (Deare) wherefore*
> *I do write of thee no more:*
> *I must answer (Sweet) thy part*
> *Lesse is here, then in my heart.*

There are quite substantial indications in Herrick's work that he did in fact have a love affair with Tomasin and that a child was born.

In 'The suspition upon his over-much familiarity with a Gentlewoman', he writes :

> *And must we part, because some say,*
> *Loud is our love, and loose our play,*
> *And more then well becomes the day?*
> *Alas for pitty! and for us*
> *Most innocent, and injur'd thus.*
> *Had we kept close, or play'd within,*
> *Suspition now had been the sinne,*
> *And shame had follow'd long ere this,*
> *T'ave plagu'd, what now unpunisht is.*
> *But we as fearlesse of the Sunne,*
> *As faultlesse; will not wish undone,*
> *What now is done: since* where no sin
> Unbolts the doore, no shame comes in.
> *Then comely and most fragrant Maid,*
> *Be you more warie, then afraid*
> *Of these Reports; because you see*
> *The fairest most suspected be.*
> *The common formes have no one eye,*
> *Or eare of burning jealousie*
> *To follow them: but chiefly, where*

Love makes the cheek, and chin a sphere
To dance and play in: (Trust me) there
Suspicion questions every haire.
Come, you are faire; and sho'd be seen
While you are in your sprightfull green:
And what though you had been embrac't
By me, were you for that unchast?
No, no, no more then is yond' Moone,
Which shining in her perfect Noone;
In all that great and glorious light,
Continues cold, as is the night.
Then, beauteous Maid, you may retire;
And as for me, my chast desire
Shall move t'wards you; although I see
Your face no more: So live you free
From Fames black lips, as you from me.

The wording is typically ambiguous. Strong evidence appears in his poem : 'Mr Hericke his daughter's Dowrye.'[1] The poem begins :

Ere I goe hence and bee noe more
Seene to the world, Ile give the skore
I owe vnto A female Child . . .

He later admonishes his daughter to prize Bashfullnes, fly the dartes of Lust, and bring A Mayden head to her wedding bed.

The Westminster where Herrick was then living was a silent city compared with noisy, turbulent London. In it stood the Abbey, St Margaret's, Parliament, Westminster Hall and St James's Palace, the seat of power of the King and his servants, later of the rulers of the Commonwealth.

The district of the Almonry, often called the Ambry, mentioned in the note by William Dell, was divided into two sections, the Great Almonry and the Little Almonry. The Great Almonry consisted of two oblong parts parallel to the two Tothill Streets and connected together by a narrow lane with an entrance from Dean's Yard. The Little Almonry ran southwards at the eastern end of Great Almonry. At the lower

1. In the Harvard manuscript this poem is headed *my* (*the* erased) *Daughter's Dowry.*

end was St Anne's Chapel and against this building stood almshouses converted into lodgings called Choristers Rents, for the singing men of the Abbey. It was a musical district and here lived William Lawes, Herrick's friend of long standing (see plate 28). The site is at the junction of what are now Victoria Street and Great Smith Street.

In the neighbourhood was a Blue Coat School and Saint Margaret's Burying Ground with its chapel. Many famous men lived and worked in this small crowded section of Westminster. Caxton had lived there earlier when his printing press was set up and in 1659, when Herrick was living in the district for a second time before his return to Dean Prior at the Restoration, Henry Purcell was born in St Ann's Lane.

Aubrey in his *Lives*, writes of another resident of the area :

> James Harrington King Charles' attendent, on the scaffold with him, for above twenty years before he died (except his imprisonment) lived in the Little Ambry, a faire house on the left hand, which looks into the Dean's Yard in Westminster. In the upper storey he had a pretty gallery, which looked into the Yard, where he commonly dined, and meditated, and took his tobacco.

Herrick had long had family connexions with Westminster[2] – his niece was buried there (see pp. 98, 99) and his brother William, her father, who died in 1632, had lived there for many years. From his apprenticeship days he had obviously been in constant contact with its residents. His friends there were numerous. Among them was Herrick's 'worthy friend', Thomas Falconbridge, appointed auditor of accounts of the Commissioners of Excise 1641–3 and later the Receiver General at Westminster, and Herrick wrote his daughter, Margaret, a Valentine while she was a little girl. Another lady to receive tribute from him was Katherine Bradshaw, the daughter of John Bradshaw, now in her twenties and the subject of a poem 'To Mistresse Katherine Bradshaw', 'the lovely, that crowned him with Laurel'.

---

2. As we have seen, Sir William Herrick lived some of his time there. (He died in 1652.)

Against this background of Westminster Herrick was to spend a short period during his absence from Devonshire and it was here that he probably spent thirteen years from 1647 until 1660 when he was ejected from his living (see page 96).

During the 1640s the land of England had long been poised for the tumult of a Civil War. That war was eventually to encompass Herrick:

'Upon the troublesome times'

O! times most bad,
Without the scope
Of hope
Of better to be had!

Where shall I goe,
Or whither run
To shun
This publique overthrow?

No places are
(This I am sure)
Secure
In this our wasting Warre.

Some storms w'ave past;
Yet we must all
Down fall,
And perish at the last.

Like most of the nobility and much of the gentry, Herrick
was an out-and-out Royalist. Everything he celebrated in life,
festivals, women, drink, were obviously sympathetic to the
Cavalier spirit and thoroughly averse to the Puritan. He
venerated Charles I and persisted in calling him the 'best of
princes' and a 'universal genius' during the gravest moments
of the Civil War when the tide was turning against the King's
men. On the eve of the Battle of Naseby, he announced his
enthusiastic act of faith in the King on a minor event, the
taking of Leicester. When Exeter was seized by Fairfax at the
beginning of 1645 he sent Sir John Berkeley, the Governor, a
poem of encouragement calling him the 'Hector of Aged
Exeter'.

Herrick was born into a world which for his class seemed
ordered – a balanced society in a balanced universe. Power
came from the centre, the court, through the aristocracy to
the merchant classes and professions down through the tradesmen and artisans to the poor. The concept of progress did not
enter men's thoughts. Life seemed static and man was formed
by God to represent the universal divine order of society. This
balance had been disturbed, thrown out of equilibrium by the
Civil War. It must have seemed to him as if chaos had inter-
penetrated the fabric of life like a destructive worm. Herrick
not only believed in the established political order but also like
Juvenal and other Roman writers he considered that his life
should be brought 'under the governance of reason'. It must
have seemed to him that reason had gone haywire.

The cult of monarchy was both real and at the same time
contrived for Herrick as for his contemporaries. He needed a
symbol to worship, and the object of his devotion was the

incumbent of the throne of England. That object of false flattery and true loyalty was soon to fall.

During Herrick's early manhood many thought there was no longer a need for a heavenly sphere.[1] A strange anxiety had appeared. It is expressed by Donne in 'An Anatomie of the World' :

> *And new Philosophy calls all in doubt,*
> *The Element of fire is quite put out;*
> *The sun is lost, and th'earth, and no mans wit*
> *Can well direct him where to look for it.*

And the sun also symbolized Kingship. Seventeenth-century man was self-questioning, doubtful of what his forefathers thought was true and secure, and often given to a sense of utter disillusion with life.

The Anglican Church, which Herrick served through most of his life, was a somewhat incongruous, but typically English, compromise. Many of its doctrines were Calvinistic while its organization and its service were strongly Catholic in character. It was flexible but vulnerable, being the middle ground between two ideals. Outside this ground Catholics said the Reformation was a sin against God and the Puritans, who wanted a return to the traditions of the early Church, based on individual conscience rather than on authority, believed reform had not advanced far enough.

Of the two poles within the Anglican Church Herrick veered for the most part towards the traditional, more Catholic wing. Herrick's Anglicanism is an essential part of his poetic canon. Like others of his time he was to inherit a great world system of thought and vision which S. Musgrove[2] describes as 'that hieratical cosmology which his century inherited from the Middle Ages and turned to such splendid public use'. Elizabeth had tried to prevent the Church being identified with any one doctrine but under James I the Church's precarious unity was diminished and the Puritans were driven out. Now during the reign of Charles, Archbishop Laud had made

1. Thomas Digge's paraphrase of Copernicus' theory that the earth moved round the sun appeared in 1576.
2. *The Universe of Robert Herrick.*

it into a minority organization. Extreme factions were ever on the alert to take over. The time of strife was at hand. This disintegration was to affect Herrick's life profoundly, as indeed it was to affect the existences of all Englishmen.

No doubt he took his misfortunes with equanimity, as he writes of his ideal reaction to disasters:

> *Give me a man that is not dull,*
> *When all the world with rifts is full:*
> *But unmaz'd dares clearly sing,*
> *When as the roof's a tottering . . .*[3]

But there were many hardships and divisions to bear. His family, as many others, was split into opposite camps. Sir William Herrick was for the established church, his two elder sons were Royalists, seeing Charles, as Herrick did, as 'an adored Caesar', while his third son, Richard, was a true Puritan.

In the War Lord Hopton brought the Royalists success in Cornwall and Herrick wrote a four line poem in his honour.

The chief Royalist stronghold in Devon was Exeter. It was finally surrendered to the Puritans in the spring of 1640. Devon as a whole had long been a Puritan stronghold and since the start of the Civil War Royalist clergy had been continually ejected from their parishes. One Puritan in Exeter, Ignatius Jourdain, promoted a bill to punish adultery by death. A climate of opinion which brought forth such men as Jourdain was naturally not favourably inclined to easy going clerics like Herrick.

The year Herrick was ejected (1647) was the point in time when Thomas Ford arrived in Devon to organize the county on Presbyterian lines. Herrick was deprived of his living by John Syms who took his place in 1648.[4] Herrick must have felt sadness in leaving his housekeeper Prue and no doubt he was loath to leave his numerous pets behind, but his cry was

---

3. 'His desire'.
4. John Weekes did not leave his parish in North Devon until a later date. There has been some speculation on the part of some of Herrick's biographers that Herrick must have joined him before returning to London but the evidence is scant.

one of triumph when he knew he was return to his birthplace and see those of his friends who were still alive.

'His returne to London'

From the dull confines of the drooping West,
To see the day spring from the pregnant East,
Ravisht in spirit, I come, nay more, I flie
To thee, blest place of my Nativitie!
Thus, thus with hallowed foot I touch the ground,
With thousand blessings by thy Fortune crown'd.
O fruitfull Genius! that bestowest here
An everlasting plenty, yeere by yeere.
O Place! O People! *Manners! fram'd to please*
All Nations, Customes, Kindreds, Languages!
I am a free-born Roman; *suffer then,*
That I amongst you live a Citizen.
London my home is: though by hard fate sent
Into a long and irksome banishment;
Yet since cal'd back; henceforward let me be,
O native countrey, repossest by thee!
For, rather then I'le to the West return,
I'le beg of thee first here to have mine Urn.
Weak I am grown, and must in short time fall;
Give thou my sacred Reliques Buriall.

11 Like to a Bride come forth my Book at last

In the midst of this period of flux in his life *Hesperides* was published. Herrick had forty years of poetry awaiting print. The year was 1648 and he was fifty-seven. The printers were John Williams and Francis Eglesfield.

Comparing the verse printed in *Hesperides* with earlier versions in manuscripts and in print issued before its appearance an observer can see how carefully he revised and polished his work. He was near his birthplace, doing a great deal of proof-reading. He also made stop-press corrections and gave a list of errata. The disciple of Ben Jonson was a meticulous and careful craftsman.

Williams ran a shop called The Crown, and Eglesfield, who made money from publishing religious works, did business at the Marigold. Both were in St Paul's Churchyard. Churchyards were the favourite places for setting up presses and St Paul's was the main area for publishing in London.[1]

Herrick also had an arrangement with Thomas Hunt, a printer in the cathedral yard in Exeter, whereby Hunt took a number of copies and put his own imprint on them. It was assumed that Herrick's friends and acquaintances in the West would be buyers. It seems that Herrick possessed some of the astute business acumen so typical of his family.

The title suggests that Herrick's poems are not only the neo-classic golden apples of the sun which gave eternal youth, but also the fruits (at least in part) of Devonshire. It is also possible to think of the poems as representing the daughters

1. By 1582 there were 175 booksellers in London of whom twenty-two were actual printers. During the seventeenth-century the numbers increased. It has been estimated during that century there were more booksellers in London than at any time before or since.

HESPERIDES:
OR,
THE WORKS
BOTH
HUMANE & DIVINE
OF
ROBERT HERRICK *Esq.*

O V I D.

Effugient avidos Carmina noſtra Rogos.

L O N D O N,

Printed for *John Williams,* and *Francis Eglesfield,*
and are to be ſold at the Crown and Marygold
in Saint *Pauls* Church-yard.   1648.

of Hesperus, the evening star; that they are in fact all small stars. The Hesperides or the Western Maidens were according to various legends three, four or even seven in number. The four named are Aegle, Erythia, Vesta and Arethusa (or Hesperis). The myth runs that Earth presented Juno with branches bearing golden apples as a wedding present for her marriage to Jupiter. Juno had them planted in a garden known as Hesperides and appointed nymphs to guard them. This garden abounded with fruits of the most delicious kinds and it was, in its turn, guarded by a dragon, Ladon, which was ever watchful and never slept. This creature was supposed to be the offspring of the giant Typhon and, like his father, he had one hundred heads and the same number of voices.

Hesiod made out the Hesperides nymphs to be the daughters of Erebus, the son of Chaos and Darkness, and Night. Diodorus Siculus (later to be followed by Milton in *Comus*) wrote of them as the daughters of Atlas and his niece, Hesperis, the daughter of Hesperus.

The garden of the Hesperides is given various sites by different authors but all agree that it was situated in the West where the Sun sets.

This large collection of his verse is in itself a monument of large proportions, created by its author to be immortal.

As other authors, he went through periods of doubt and times of certainty in his feelings towards his work :

> *I cannot pipe as I was wont to do*
> *Broke is my Reed, hoarse is my singing too . . .*[2]

and

'Not every day fit for Verse'

> *'Tis not ev'ry day, that I*
> *Fitted am to prophesie:*
> *No, but when the Spirit fils*
> *The fantastick Pannicles:*
> *Full of fier; then I write*
> *As the Godhead doth indite.*

2. 'The Poet hath lost his pipe'.

Thus inrag'd, my lines are hurl'd,
Like the Sybells, *through the world.*
Look how next the holy fier,
Either slakes, or doth retire;
So the Fancie cooles, till when
That brave Spirit comes agen.

However, it was more frequent that he addressed his book as an immortal work with such descriptions as 'richest jewels over-cast' or as 'a plant sprung up to wither never'.

Hesperides is viewed as work in its own right by T. S. Eliot in *What is minor Poetry?* :[3] '. . . we also get the feeling of a unifying personality, and we get to know this personality better by reading all of his poems, and for having read all of his poems we enjoy still better the ones we like best. But first, there is no such continuous conscious *purpose* about Herrick's poems; he is more the purely natural and un-selfconscious man, writing his poems as the fancy seizes him; and second, the personality expressed in them is less unusual – in fact, it is its honest *ordinariness* which gives the charm. Relatively, we get much more of him from one poem than we do of Herbert from one poem : still there is *something* more in the whole than in the parts."

That 'something' is the presence of Herrick, the stuff of his own making. *Hesperides,* though untidy like any man's character, contains strands which though not united, combine to make an entity and Herrick puts a characteristic stamp on practically every line he wrote. Thus, like Horace's *Carmina,* the poems in *Hesperides* are arranged in 'that orderly disorder common in Nature', as Ben Jonson put it. A lyric song is placed next to a coarse epigram. The range of theme and character is wide; the pastoral, cynical, vulgar, learned, moral, the elegaic and freshly simple, the didactic and the rococo, drama in the masque form, are all jumbled together. The Christian and the pagan are sometimes fused into one conception. Modern scholars have shown however that *Hesperides* has a chronological purpose. Perhaps he took a real 'delight in disorder' in order to produce variety and he doubtless interspersed his sweet, trivial, pretty poems as well as his more

3. *The Sewanee Review,* Vol. LIV, No. 1, 1946.

serious verse with crude epigrams as a counterbalance to avoid a cloying effect.

The student of Herrick, as T. S. Eliot suggests, should read his verse as a whole but the average present-day reader with little time would best enjoy his work in selection. Taken from the body of *Hesperides*, his finest poems may be slightly out of context, show only certain bright qualities, but such a distillation of his verse the more clearly demonstrates his genius as a lyricist.

He was at last in print but he was without a living and the
country was ruled by a government for which Herrick could
only feel fear and dislike.

John Walker in *Sufferings of the Clergy*,[1] 1714, writes of
Herrick: 'He was a Sober and Learned Man; and was
Presented to his Living by his Majesty King Charles I on the
Promotion of Dr Potter to the See of Carlisle; and having no
Fifths paid him, was subsisted by Charity, until the Restora-
tion: at which time he returned to this Viccaridge.'

His income must have indeed stopped when he left Dean
Prior but it must not be concluded that the help he received
was insufficient. He had distinguished relations to whom he
had wisely dedicated poems. The unswerving Royalist no
doubt received aid from those who had kept loyal to Charles.
Ann, his maternal aunt, had married into the Soane family
and there were others of influence and wealth.

It is not known definitely what Herrick was doing during
the Commonwealth but it would seem that he was living again
in Westminster. Anthony à Wood wrote that he was living in
'St Anne's parish'. There was no parish of this name during
Herrick's day but Wood is probably referring to St Anne's
Street and Lane in St Margaret's parish. St Anne's Street and
Lane which took their name from the chapel were near the
Little Almonry. It would be a natural place for him to live.
He had lived in the district before and here his friends were
living.

This time of his return to lay dress is really no more than
a gap of thirteen years in which we have not even the vaguest
strands of information for speculation. It must have been not

1. Under *The Parochial Clergy*, p. 263.

only a time of uncertainty for him but possibly of anguish, as he wrote 'To his Friend, on the untuneable Times':

Griefe, (my deare friend) has first Harp unstung;
Wither'd my hand, and palsie-struck my tongue.

He was already well into middle age and presumably without employment. His work did appear sporadically after the publication of *Hesperides*, but not in a flattering light.

Once again Herrick is a ghost moving against a speculative topographical background with only the spirit of the times to fit him into any place.

*   *

In June 1660, less than a month after Charles II returned to England, the new House of Lords ordered all tithes in Puritan parishes to be held by the churchwardens until they could be returned to the former incumbents.

One of the first petitions addressed to 'the right honourable the Lords in Parlyament Assembled' was from Herrick:

The humble peticion of Robert Herricke (Clerke *erased*) Vicar of Deane prior in the County of Devon Sheweth That the Vicaridge aforesayd hath bin for Divers yeares sequestred from your Peticioner for the affection that he bore to his late Majesty of blessed Memory. Your Peticioner humbly prayes That the Tythes, Glebes, and all other profitts belonging to the (Rectory afores *erased*) Vicaridge aforesayd may be secured & sequestred in the hands of the Churchwardens or Overseers of the poore of the parish aforesayd untill your peticioner doe prove his Tytle by Lawe.

And your peticioner shall ever pray &c
Robert Herrick

13   Return to Dean Prior

Public transport had become more widespread during the Commonwealth. In the year of Cromwell's death, 1658, the first stage coaches set out from the George Inn, Aldersgate, to various cities throughout the country. The journey to Exeter, which now took four days, cost forty shillings and to Plymouth fifty shillings. We can only hope that the return journey to Dean Prior which Herrick had to make in 1660 at the age of sixty-nine was more comfortable than his previous travelling from London to South Devon must have been.

One hundred and forty-two clergymen had been ejected from Devon during the Commonwealth. Herrick was among the one hundred and twenty-one who were restored. He replaced John Syms, a staunch Presbyterian who went on preaching his doctrine in his own house and in the neighbouring villages after his ejection.

Some returning vicars were fêted, for in certain parts of Devon the Restoration was greeted with enthusiasm. In Exeter the conduits are said to have run with wine. It is unknown how Herrick was received. One can only surmise that it was a mixed welcome, for Syms must have had his staunch followers. Prudence Baldwin returned to his service, and there must have been comfort in their reunion.

Though no doubt he felt some content he must have regretted leaving London and one can imagine his sadness when in 1666, old and infirm,[1] he heard of the devastation during the Great Fire.

He was certainly remembered in the village long after his

1. In the 1660s the records of the births and deaths in the Dean Prior register are signed by an infirm hand.

death. In *The Quarterly Review*, August 1810, in a review of a selection of his poems published that year by Longmans, Barron Field wrote of his visit to Dean Prior 'last summer' (i.e. 1809, 136 years after Herrick's death):

We found many persons in the village who could repeat some of his lines, and none who were not acquainted with his *Farewell to Dean Bourn*

> *Dean Bourn farewell; I never look to see*
> *Dean, or thy warty incivility.*

which they said, he uttered as he crossed the brook, upon being ejected by Cromwell from the vicarage, to which he had been presented by Charles I. 'But,' they added, with an air of innocent triumph, *'he did see it again'*; as was the fact, after the Restoration. And, indeed, although he calls Devonshire 'dull', yet as he admits, at the same time, that 'he never invented such ennobled numbers for the press, as in that loathed spot', the good people of Dean Prior have not much reason to be dissatisfied.

The person, however, who knows more of Herrick than all the rest of the neighbourhood, we found to be a poor woman in the ninety-ninth year of her age, [i.e. born 1710] named Dorothy King. She repeated to us, with great exactness, five of his 'Noble Numbers', among which was the beautiful Litany quoted above ['To the Holy Spirit']. These she had learned from her mother, who was apprenticed to Herrick's successor in the vicarage. She called them her prayers, which, she said, she was in the habit of putting up in bed, whenever she could not sleep; and she therefore began the Litany at the second stanza,

> *When I lie within my bed, &c.*

Another of her midnight orisons was the poem beginning

> *Every night thou dost me fright,*
> *And keep mine eyes from sleeping, &c.*

She had no idea that these poems had ever been printed, and could not have read them if she had seen them. She is in possession of few traditions as to the person, manners, and habits of life of the poet; but in return, she has a whole budget of anecdotes respecting his ghost; and these she details with a careless but serene gravity, which one would not willingly discompose by any hints at a remote possibility of their not being exactly true. Herrick, she says, was a bachelor, and kept a maid-servant, as his poems indeed discover; but she adds, what they do not discover, that he also kept a pet-pig, which he taught to drink out of a tankard. And this important circumstance, together with a tradition that he one day threw his sermon at the congregation, with a curse for their inattention, forms almost the sum total of what we could collect of the poet's life.

During this latter period of his life, in fact since the appearance of *Hesperides*, Herrick appears to have written virtually nothing except for 'The New Charon' upon the death of Lord Hastings, set by Henry Lawes (1649), and, according to John Prince in *Danomonii Orientales Illustres*, 1701, he wrote while 'very aged' the epitaph on the tomb of Sir Edward Giles, who died in 1642, and his wife, which is placed on the wall of the south aisle of Dean Prior Church. The last two lines mean that Herrick felt he was approaching near his death when he wrote the poem :

> *These Two asleep are: I'll be Undrest*
> *and so to Bed: Pray wish us all Good Rest.*

The parish register at Dean Prior reports : 'Robert Herrick Vicker was buried yᵉ 15ᵗʰ day of October – 1674'.

Few memorials remain to Herrick in his native London. There is a street named after him in Westminster, situated at the back of the Tate Gallery, parallel with John Islip Street, and another, Herrick Road in Highbury.

In St Margaret's, Westminster a new plaque has been erected in place of the original in memory of Mistris Elizabeth Herrick (see page 79), the daughter of William, and Herrick's niece, who died and was buried in 1630 at the age of eleven.

She had previously been christened in the church. Stow, in his 1633 edition, mentions the original plaque as placed on the wall at the lower end of the north aisle.

On the present plaque these words precede the quotation : 'This epitaph of Robert Herrick formerly on a mural tablet in the middle of the north aisle of this church, was restored in memory of James Rumsey whom the State of West Virginia honours as the inventor of the steamboat, which he demonstrated privately to George Washington in 1784 and publicly on The Potomac River at Shepherdstown W. Va. 3 December 1787. Born of English parents in Cecil County, Maryland in 1743, he died while lecturing on the principles of steam navigation to English scientists in London, and was buried in St Margaret's Churchyard 24 December 1792.'

> *Sweet virgin, that I do not set*
> *The pillars up of weeping* Jet,
> *Or mournfull* Marble; *let thy shade*
> *Not wrathfull seem, or fright the Maide,*
> *Who hither at her wonted howers*
> *Shall come to strew thy earth with flowers.*
> *No, know (Blest Maide) when there's not one*
> *Remainder left of Brasse or stone,*
> *Thy living Epitaph shall be,*
> *Though lost in them, yet found in me.*
> *Dear, in they bed of Roses, then,*
> *Till this world shall dissolve as men,*
> *Sleep, while we hide thee from the light,*
> *Drawing thy curtains round:* Good night.

Nearby in the Abbey in Poets' Corner stands another plaque in a relief with masks at the base; on it is written :

O RARE BEN : JOHNSON

14 *Upon himselfe*

What was this man whose bones lie somewhere in the grave-yard of Dean Prior church really like? Of his critics and biographers, F. Delattre and Walter de la Mare come nearest to what could seem to be some of the true aspects of Herrick's nature.

De la Mare[1] writes that Herrick was humble, loved the familiar, and disliked all pomp and pretentiousness, that he was neither a hypocrite nor a fanatic. He was a humane and charitable man and he did not lack courage, but he was not heroic. These qualities, writes de la Mare, go to make an English gentleman. One could add to this assessment that another quality which was typical of Herrick's Englishness was his great love of animals.

Delattre[2] finds him soft and charming, and in contrast, at times Rabelaisian. He is equaniminous: '*Sa colère s'achève presque toujours en un éclat de rire.*' He has a sensual imagination and while he remains in the sphere of sensations and sensuality he is an exquisite poet.[3] But, writes Delattre, the man does not match up to his work. Herrick is '*un grand enfant parfois*'.

Clues to Herrick's real character in his verse are few and often contradictory. So the qualities of the essential man remain somewhat obscure. Many ambiguities lie between the clergy-man, the man of letters versed in the Classics, and the hedonist.

1. *The Bookman*, 1908.
2. *Robert Herrick*, 1912.
3. Delattre writes a little later: '*C'est un connaisseur minutieux, habile à définer l'éclat d'une fleure, ou le parfum qui s'exhale d'une robe de femme.*'

Mary Lascelles said in a broadcast[4] : 'For a poet who talks about himself so much so freely and with such apparent candour, Herrick tells uncommonly little.'

Herrick's reserve is commensurate with the theme he is treating. He is often frank and witty about his love of drinking but whether he was convivial and a good companion alone, again is uncertain. Did he drink to hide from reality to any great degree? His 'A Hymne to Bacchus' may well indicate that at one time in his life drinking had become a problem for him :

> BACCHUS, let me drink no more;
> Wild are Seas, that want a shore
> When our drinking has no stint,
> There is no pleasure in't.
> I have drank up for to please
> Thee, that great cup Hercules:
> Urge no more; and there shall be
> Daffadills g'en up to Thee.

Herrick is both contradictory and evasive about his relationship with women, an understandable trait in a bachelor parson. He was not the only poet of his time to write in the Anacreonistic spirit of the day. Many Elizabethan and Jacobean poets dedicated their verses to non-existent mistresses. Cowley's pen extols the charms of no less than twenty-one, but he was, in fact, too shy to even speak of love to a woman. Verse confessions were in fact a traditional literary form for the English of this time, as they had been for the Greeks and Romans. The large number of mistresses who are the objects of Herrick's love poems are of no real significance for a biographer.

Herrick is sometimes portrayed as a Cavalier poet who courts love itself rather than women, a man who never wrote passionately nor ever knew passion. This is not wholly true, but he did have a moderate side to his nature and he expresses sensuality in his poetry by what he himself terms a 'cleanly wantonness'. At his best he can create an ambience very similar in atmosphere to the eighteenth-century French paintings of Boucher and Fragonard :

4. On the Third Programme in the series 'The Art of Poetry—7' on 18 April 1949.

'Her Legs'

Fain would I kiss my Julia's Leg,
Which is as white and hairless as an egge.

and

'To the Western wind'

Sweet Western Wind, whose luck it is,
(Made rivall with the aire)
To give Perenn'as *lip a kisse,*
And fan her wanton haire.

Bring me but one, Ile promise thee,
Instead of common showers,
Thy wings shall be embalm'd by me
And all beset with flowers.

Most of his imagined women are subtle, sensual, mezzotint creatures, rather than actual people. But though much of his verse to women has some of the delicacy of French seventeenth-century lyrics, his protests are sometimes merely quaint and coy. They can have a delicate but false ring:

'The shoe tying'

Anthea *bade me tye her shooe;*
I did; and kist the Instep too:
And would have kist unto her knee,
Had not her Blush rebuked me.

and when in this vein he can be delicate but at the same time ridiculous:

'How Roses came red'

1 *Roses at first were white,*
   Till they co'd not agree,
   Whether my Sapho's *breast,*
   Or they more white sho'd be.

2 *But being vanquisht quite,*
   A blush their cheeks bespred;

102

Since which (beleeve the rest)
The Roses *first came red.*

One also suspects that, though in a language with an
accidental twentieth-century flavour he writes that we should :

Kisse our Dollies night and day

one is also reminded in poems like 'The Vision to Electra' that
he might in fact have lacked love in reality and that his sensual
feelings must have been mostly confined to his fantasy :

I dream'd we both were in a bed
Of Roses, almost smothered:
The warmth and sweetnes had me there
Made lovingly familiar:
But that I heard thy sweet breath say,
Faults done by night, will blush by day:
I kist thee (panting,) and I call
Night to the Record! that was all.
But ah! if empty dreames so please,
Love give me more such nights as these.

Perhaps he was not attractive to women, except to Tomasin,
at any time in his life. One senses in his verse that he might well
have been ungainly and clumsy. Was this a reason why he
drank a great deal? Here one is in the domain of speculation
and to analyse Herrick through traits appearing to arise in his
verse is a fruitless task. He was hypersensitive to smells and
perfumes and writes constantly about them. But this frequent
reference to smell might well be a natural preoccupation of
any man of the time when houses and streets were constantly
sprinkled with herbs and flowers to banish stench. Scents,
too, were thought to ward off the plague. Sweet smells
were a luxury, an exception to the unpleasant everyday
stink.

One can sense some of the flavour of Herrick in his work,
but one gains little reward in trying to delve into his personality
from an analytical standpoint. It would be equally fruitless to
suggest homosexual traits in his verse to men in which he

103

declares his love and devotion. The attitudes and expressions are no more than convention, though they were meant, too, to express sincere friendship. It is fruitless to judge Herrick by any twentieth-century psychoanalytical criteria.

Sometimes, though, he can express his sensual feelings quite openly. In 'The Vine', he is sensual to a degree which cannot hide that he would at least wish to be voluptuous.

> *I dream'd this mortal part of mine*
> *Was Metamorphoz'd to a Vine;*
> *Which crawling one and every way,*
> *Enthrall'd my dainty Lucia.*
> *Me thought, her long small legs & thighs*
> *I with my Tendrils did surprize;*
> *Her Belly, Buttocks, and her Waste*
> *By my soft Nerv'lits were embrac'd . . .*

Like Ovid's Corinna, Herrick's mistresses are often composite figures of several women and none of them has a consistent personality. They have Latinate names and their attributes are again classical conceits – they tend in the main to be stately, sweet and smooth skinned.

Julia, however, is rather different. In his poems written to her Herrick appears to be more realistic in approach, and she seems more vivid to us than the others. In 'Upon his Julia', he writes that her eye is 'black and rolling', and that she is double-chinned and has a high forehead, red lips, cheeks like 'Creame Enclarited' and a graceful nose. Elsewhere he describes her as wearing rich silks, deep coloured satins and a dark blue petticoat which on one occasion was starred with gold. He also writes that she is buxom and her hair, which he himself braids, is bright and dewy. The poems to Julia such as 'Upon Julia's unlacing herself' are for the most part more erotic than his love poems addressed to other names.

'Upon Julia's unlacing her self'

> *Tell, if thou canst, (and truly) whence doth come*
> *This Camphire, Storax, Spiknard, Galbanum:*
> *These Musks, these Ambers, and those other smells*

(Sweet as the Vestrie of the Oracles.*)*
Ile tell thee; while my Julia *did unlace*
Her silken bodies, but a breathing space:
The passive Aire such odour then assum'd,
As when to Jove *Great* Juno *goes perfum'd.*
Whose pure-Immortall body doth transmit
A scent, that fills both Heaven and Earth with it.

The more one looks into the Julia poems the more one is convinced that some woman or other seems to stand behind the façade. One possibility is that Julia is a composite portrait of all the women he loved. Not a few writers, including Edith Sitwell, Walter de la Mare and Humbert Wolfe, have thought that she must have actually lived.

Professor Saintsbury, in his *History of English Literature* writes : 'I believe that the warmest of the Julia poems are written in the same integrity' and Edmund Gosse even speculates that Herrick must have met Julia in his youth and that she died or disappeared before he left Cambridge. He even supposes that she might have been the woman, Tomasin, who bore him an illegitimate daughter.

Whether these conjectures have any validity or no, Julia does seem more alive, not only to his readers, but to Herrick too, though even of her he confesses :

Mine eye and heart
Dotes less on nature than on art.

To say the least, Herrick is very contradictory about his love life. In the last two lines of 'The Pillar of Fame', the last poem in *Hesperides,* he writes :

To his Book's end this last line he'd have plac't,
Jocund his Muse was; but his Life was chast.

This thought, however, follows a classical convention and this assertion is not necessarily true at all. It is found in several classical authors including Catullus. Ovid (Trist ii 354), from whom it seems Herrick borrowed directly in this case, writes :
Vita verecunda est, Musa iocosa mea

Five short poems earlier in *Hesperides* Herrick again echoes Ovid (Trist ii 213 and elsewhere) in 'On Himselfe' :

> *Il'e write no more of Love; but now repent*
> *Of all the times that I in it have spent . . .*

These lines seem to be those of a clergyman regretting his profane thoughts before the publication of his two works. The second book, *His Noble Numbers*, which celebrate God and Christ would seem to be some sort of atonement. Even more contradictions are found in *Hesperides* :

'Upon Himselfe'

> *Mop-ey'd, I am, as some have said,*
> *Because I've liv'd so long a maid: . . .*

'To his Tomb-maker'

> *. . . Chaste I liv'd, without a wife*
> *That's the story of my life . . .*

and

'Poets'

> *Wantons we are; and though our words be such*
> *Our lives do differ from our Lines by much.*

He frequently reveals himself as a misogynist in his work and this can well be true. He can be completely cynical in his attitude towards women :

'Upon some women'

> *Thou who wilt not love, doe this;*
> *Learne of me what Woman is.*
> *Something made of thred and thrumme;*
> *A merre Botch of all and some.*
> *Pieces, patches, ropes of haire;*
> *Inlaid Garbage ev'ry where.*

Out-side silk, and out-side Lawne;
Sceanes[5] to cheat us neatly drawne.
False in legs and false in thighes;
False in breast, teeth, haire, and eyes:
False in head, and false enough;
Onely true in shreds and stuffe.

In one respect, however, there can be little doubt about his stance.

Perhaps one of the most important aspects of the man was that he was an out and out conformist both in his life and his work. His verse is not particularly innovatory and his own instincts and attitudes were towards the established order. The Church of England and the throne were natural institutions not only to be accepted but to be praised.

He conformed and rejoiced in the society into which he was born and when that world began to crumble he managed to survive without compromising his principles and returned eventually to his calling after the Restoration.

Another aspect of his nature is also beyond doubt. He is not, as many critics have maintained, merely a pleasant trifler. His real self lies, according to circumstance, somewhere between the many gradations of the light and the serious, and his personality was a flexible and balanced one.

Yet when all is said and done, a search into his true nature does not bring one much further than what is revealed by the bust in the Marshall engraving: a robust and somewhat ungainly man who would wish to play the part of an Englishman dresed in a toga against a backdrop of the Hill of Parnassus, a poet rejoicing a little sadly at the spring in the Sacred Grove. His poise is incongruous but it is of such incongruity as this that the stuff of poetry sometimes emerges.

The next chapters will trace a path through a landscape created by his own particular conception of the Helicon gardens and tell of his tributes to the fountain Hippocrene, so sacred to the Muses.

5. Sceanes = curtains, veils.

15   A Goblet to Ovid and a Cup to Catullus

CRWNO

At the beginning of Elizabeth's reign England had been a cultural backwater in comparison with much of Europe, particularly with Italy and France. The impact of European Renaissance culture on England and what could be termed her own culture both reached a stage of fruition during the age of Shakespeare and Jacobean England; in fact during Herrick's lifetime.

These two impacts are present in his verse, but it is above all the intrinsic classical qualities of Renaissance literature which are dominant.

Herrick evokes the Roman gods, presents Christian ritual in terms of Roman sacrifices. His mistresses have Roman names. His vocabulary itself is highly Latinate[1] but he introduces his Latinisms among homely Anglo-Saxon words to make telling phrases as 'Fleshie Principalities'.

His essential English qualities did not escape Gerard Manley Hopkins[2]. In a letter to Robert Bridges (14 August 1879), Hopkins writes : 'His (Barnes') poems use to charm me also by their Westcountry "instress", a most peculiar product of England, which I associate with airs like Weeping Winefred, Polly Oliver, or Poor Mary Ann with Herrick and Herbert . . . and above all with the smell of oxeyes and applelofts . . .'

The flavour of his verse, his temperament and attitudes are, however, often profoundly Augustan. In his earlier work he draws on Catullus and above all Horace, and his later verse, which tends to be more economical in its execution, on Ovid

1. Supremest = last; convinces = will conquer; retorted = drawn back; prime = the beginning; determines = ends; dulce = sweetly.
2. *The Letters of Gerard Manley Hopkins to Robert Bridges*, O.U.P., 1935.

(above all for his love poetry), Martial and Tacitus. In general, the greatest influence is from Horace, though this effect does not necessarily come direct from the Roman poet. His debt to Catullus and other Latin poets is freely admitted in

'To live merrily, and Trust to Good Verses' :

> *Then this immensive cup*
> *Of* Aromatike *wine,*
> Catullus, *I quaffe up*
> *To that Terce Muse of thine.*

Elsewhere in the poem he drinks a health to Homer, Virgil and Ovid, a Tun to Propertius and a 'flood' to Tibullus. His influence from these elegists can be traced, and also from Seneca and Martial. He can borrow from an ancient and then continue on a personal note.

In 'When he would have his Verses read' he is directly indebted to Martial while creating his own special originality :

> *In sober mornings, doe not thou reherse*
> *The holy incantation of a verse;*
> *But when that men have both well drunke, and fed,*
> *Let my Enchantments then be sung, or read.*

and the last two lines :

> *When the* Rose *raignes, and locks with ointments shine,*
> *Let rigid* Cato *read these Lines of mine.*

is almost direct from Martial (X, 20 (19) 20–21),

> *cum regnat rosa, cum madent capilli:*
> *tunc me vel rigidi legant Catones.*

There is little doubt he read the Flemish humanist, Jean Second (1511–36), *Elegies* Book I, from whom he may have derived the name Julia, and Jean Bonnefons (1554–1614), who was much admired by Jonson. It seems very possible that he was influenced by translation including Florio's version of

Montaigne, and he must have been indebted to Burton's *The Anatomy of Melancholy* (see page 70).

There were numerous translations made from the Latin during his day and this, together with his own education in the classics, meant that he was living perpetually within a classical climate. Moreover, he did not wish to escape the influence of this climate.

In that world of classical humanism it was above all the works of Jonson that left the most profound mark upon his work. There are Jonsonian phrases scattered throughout *Hesperides*. The 'Night Piece to Julia' recalls the Song of Patricio in 'Gipsies Metamorphos'd'. 'A Country Life : to his Brother, M. Tho : Herrick' owes much to the 'Epistle to Sir Robert Wroth', the 'Panegerick to Sir Lewis Pemberton' to 'Penshurst', and 'Delight in Disorder' is strongly reminiscent of 'Still to be neat'.

Herrick is also indebted to Jonson for some of his verse forms. The reaction against the Petrarchan tradition which began with Jonson and Donne is maintained in Herrick's work. Such forms as the sonnet are missing in the work of Jonson's nearest disciple.

Herrick found in the work of Jonson a perfectly conceived model of classicism to follow assiduously. Though less of a classical scholar than Jonson, Herrick, always a pupil at the master's side, still enters the Ancient World (mainly Roman) to an even greater degree, and is the greater improviser of the two, for he had an instinctive understanding of the Ancients' sensuality. He was to adapt the Augustans, not borrow from them. At times he even parodied them. He was a Latinist who only occasionally turned to Greece. Yet he was intrigued by the poets of the Greek Anthology, particularly by Anacreon. In Anacreon Herrick met not only a model, but a not dissimilar temperament to his own : both delighted in self portraits and were gay and fanciful. He borrows the themes of Anacreon's drinking songs and the Greek poet's influence can be detected in many of his light, short lyrics. Herrick took the images of the Greeks, as he did from the Latin poets, but he was no slavish imitator.

It is not of any real importance if he had full recourse to the original text. Greek was widely taught in schools and though

Herrick was certainly not as familiar with the Classics as Ben
Jonson, he could certainly glean the sense of a piece of Greek
verse and he does quote Hesiod on the frontispiece of his *Noble
Numbers*.

Herrick can produce lines of originality but it is as a writer
drawing his subject matter from the Classics (but not a
plagiarist), that he must be appreciated and criticized. Elizabethans and Jacobeans were complacent in their borrowings
and felt they needed no justification for translations or adap-
tations.

K. A. McEuen in *Classical Influence of the Tribe of Ben*
writes that the Ancients themselves did not interpret 'originality'
as 'invention' :

> An awareness of the preponderant classicism in the
> writings of our English poets should not make the reader
> deprecate these writers and disparage their originality.
> Rather, it should increase the admiration and appreciation
> for what these men have done . . .
>
> Making no pretence to being the very first to say a thing,
> a classical poet was content with restating an idea, providing
> he could make excellent use of it. It was with him as with
> a musical composer. A Brahms borrowing a theme from a
> Beethoven does not cease to be original : if he develops, and
> elaborates upon, that theme in his own way, the resulting
> creation is something original, standing upon its own merits.

Herrick borrows on his own terms. He transforms the original
and his poetry has its own flavour and unique quality. He is a
neo-classic poet of the first order. As Palladio translated, transformed, improvised and re-invented Classical architecture, so
Herrick on a minor scale exposed and recreated the themes
of the Classical writers.

Hesperides is constructed by an intellect and a temperament
steeped in the worlds of Ancient Rome, and to a lesser extent
that of Greece. As Roger B. Rollin writes in *Robert Herrick*
(1966) : '. . . his poems constitute a world which has an order
and a harmony that are no more blatantly obvious but no less
effectually real than the order and the harmony of the actual
universe.'

16   *A Growth to meet decay*

'The Argument of his Book'

I sing of Brooks, *of* Blossomes, Birds, *and* Bowers:
Of April, May, *of* June, *and* July-*Flowers.*
I sing of May-poles, Hock-carts, Wassails, Wakes,
Of Bride-grooms, Brides, *and of their* Bridall-cakes.
I write of Youth, *of* Love, *and have Accesse*
*By these, to sing of cleanly-*Wantonnesse.
I sing of Dewes, *of* Raines, *and piece by piece*
Of Balme, *of* Oyle, *of* Spice, *and* Amber-Greece.
I sing of Times trans-shifting; *and I write*
How Roses *first came* Red, *and* Lillies White.
I write of Groves, *of* Twilights, *and I sing*
The Court of Mab, *and of the* Fairie-King.
I write of Hell; *I sing (and ever shall)*
Of Heaven, *and hope to have it after all.*

This 'Argument' lists Herrick's poetic aims : to sing of idyllic
nature, man's pleasures, the concept of love without guilt –
'cleanly-Wantonnesse', of natural objects employed by mankind, of the passing of time – 'Times trans-shifting' – of the
faërie and lastly of his relationship with God.

    We have seen how Herrick's landscape is a cultivated one,
a garden in which he develops a complex humanity, an ideal
of civility and courtliness. This Hesperides contrasts with the
natural world which is a wilderness reflected in his anti-bucolic
poems. His gardens of the West, at times almost as artificial
as the *Arcadia* of Sidney, are formal and classical but they also
hold a wholesome English quality of fresh fields, country customs and homeliness. The context is often Mediterranean and

112

the setting English. This mixture adds reality to his fantasy, for the Classical gods walk without inconsequence throughout a green countryside. His women though, with Classic names, disguise a distant, for the most part totally unseen English original.

He has made a new Hesperides whose fruits take the shape of poems. His grand theme is a universal one and in reflecting man's nature he can be thoughtful as well as sensual. Every object in Eden does not fill him with pure delight. Many of the poems possess a wistful sadness which at times can become poignant.

Some of his flowers, like Blake's rose, can grow sick from a parasitic growth. The stalks and leaves of the plants of his Hesperides are for ever attacked by the disease of time. He also wrote of the 'untuneable times' during the Commonwealth and of time which in the end would place him in the earth:

> *Then shall my ghost not walk about, but keep*
> *Still in the cool and silent shades of sleep.*

Herrick is realistic as well as fantastic; he celebrates the good life as well as the life of idyllic fancy. Some of his tastes are simple – he loves his wort and his beetroot. He is an apologist for a harmonious life with moderate aims and a content in domestic pleasures suffuses some of his poems written in Devonshire and earlier in London. In 'A Country Life: to his Brother, M. Tho: Herrick', written when he was still young, about the year 1610, he extols the Englishman's ideal of living a cultivated life in the country, a theme much prized by Ben Jonson:

> *. . . to live round, and close, and wisely true*
> *To thine owne selfe; and knowne to few.*
> *Thus let thy Rurall sanctuary be*
> Elizium *to thy wife and thee . . .*

and he later takes up the theme in 'The Country life, to The honoured Mr. End. Porter' and 'A Panegerick to Sir Lewis Pemberton'. Such poems reflect an agreeable acceptance of a perfect reality.

Herrick's view of nature was animistic. This can be seen clearly in his flower and blossom poems. The flowers he writes about are not picked from the Devon hedgerows and fields nor from London gardens. They are planted in his own soil as symbols, for the human world is always with him as it had been with the Alexandrine poets and the Elizabethans. This symbolism was of course common throughout Rennaisance Europe. Herrick's method of seeing flowers and nature in terms of human dress and features is seen in the work of many Renaissance poets, e.g. Ronsard's *Casandre* :

> *Mignonne allons voir si la Rose*
> *Qui ce matin avoit desclose,*
> *Sa robe de pourpre au Soleil,*
> *A point perdu ceste vesperée*
> *Et son teint au vostre pareil.*

The Romantics, of course, viewed Nature from quite a different standpoint. In contrast to Wordsworth's flowers, Herrick's daffodils and blossoms are emblems of mortality. Wordsworth extols his daffodils and periwinkles for their own intrinsic qualities and significance. Yet though Herrick's flowers are symbols they do, like Wordsworth's, possess a real freshness. The freshness in Herrick's case is that of Renaissance England. So the flowers in Herrick's poems, the roses, lilies, carnations and violets are derived from early sources, unwild. In his flower poems he is close to the tradition of emblem and fable. The flowers can sometimes become personified, producing a naïve effect. A lily may be 'marryed with a maid called Rose' or violets are 'poore girles'; the effect can be fresh and inspired, and also slightly silly.

'To Violets'

> *Welcome Maids of Honour,*
> *You doe bring*
> *In the Spring;*
> *And wait upon her.*
>
> *She has Virgins many,*
> *Fresh and faire;*

114

Yet you are
More sweet then any.

Y'are the Maiden Posies,
And so grac't,
To be plac't,
'Fore Damask Roses.

Yet though thus respected,
By and by
Ye doe lie,
Poore Girles, neglected.

Northrop Frye writes in his *Anatomy of Criticism* : 'Herrick's daffodils, unlike Wordsworth's, are directly confronted, and the confronted image readily becomes personified. Here we are in an area corresponding to the masque drama, and the innocent vision and the fairyland of animistic romance return.'[1]

The human world whether real or neo-classic is always present for Herrick. Herrick, the Londoner, must have always been keenly aware of the flowers and blossoms he symbolizes. Flowers abounded in his London. John Gerard in his *Herball* published in 1597 says of the daffodil, the narcissus and 'primrose perless' : 'We have them all and everie of them in our London gardens, in great abundance – the King's Speare, or small yellow Asphodill; the White Asphodill or Daffodil; and the double white Daffodil of Constantinople.' Gerard also mentions lilies (the Persian lily), varieties of cherry, and pear and apple blosoms : 'All sorts of roses', he writes at the end of a long list, 'we have in our London gardens, except that rose without prickles'. Flowers, trees and grasses grew not only in gardens and in the grounds of the Inns of Court where many of Herrick's lawyer friends from Cambridge lived, but haphazard in open spaces throughout the town. Gerard writes that the 'wilde clarie' or 'oculus Christi' was to be seen 'especially in the fields of Holbourne, neere unto Graies Inne, in the high way, by the end of a bricke wall' and also 'at the end of Chelsey next to London'.

Herrick was familiar with the flowers he extols from his earliest days but he always sees practically everything in nature

1. Princeton, 1957, pp. 259–301.

in human terms. This animistic view of nature develops into a universal theme in Herrick's verse. The pastoral poet is not only a poet of nature. He may describe the ideal landscape and the real one but he also sees all growth in those landscapes continually decaying into oblivion. Of all the themes listed in his *Argument* that of Times trans-shifting makes the finest poetry. Herrick is there writing of a concept found in all literatures as the idea that all the world is a stage. Transcience, the 'hasting day' and the clasping of love and pleasure while they are present evoked deep emotion in Herrick. Both themes are Horatian : the *Eheu fugaces*[2] and *carpe diem* of the *Odes*. The first, as the second, has been celebrated and lamented in most cultures both Eastern and Western. The decaying of fruits, flowers, blossoms, the fate of all animate objects is a constant reminder of the mortality of man and particularly the passing beauty of women. This theme of transience is found in the works of many of the Elizabethans :

Sir Walter Raleigh (1552?–1618) in his *History of the World* : '. . . and the beauty of our youth, to the flowers of the spring, which, either in a very short time or with the sun's heat, dry up and wither away, or the fierce puffs of wind blow them from the stalks.'

Two of Herrick's best known poems are based on the concept of *Eheu fugaces*. In 'To Daffadills' human tears and dew are intermingled in the imagery :

2.   *Eheu fugaces, Postume, Postume,*
                  labuntur anni, nec pietas moram
                  rugis et instanti senectae
                  adferet indomitaeque morti; . . .

First stanza Horace *Odes* XIV Book II, translated by C. E. Bennett (Loeb's Classical Library) as

        Alas, O Postumus, Postumus, the years glide swifly by, nor will righteousness give pause to wrinkles, to advancing age, or Death invincible . . .

In 'His Age, dedicated to his peculiar friend, M John Wickes, under the name of Postumus' Herrick is very close to the actual text of Horace's poem :

          Ah Posthumus! Our yeares hence flye,
           And leave no sound; nor piety,
              Or prayers, or vow
         Can keepe the wrinkle from the brow:
               But we must on,
           As Fate do's lead or draw us; . . .

Faire Daffadills, we weep to see
You haste away so soone:
As yet the early-rising Sun
Has not attain'd his Noone.
Stay, stay,
Untill the hasting day
Has run
But to the Even-song;
And, having pray'd together, we
Will goe with you along.

We have short time to stay, as you,
We have as short a Spring;
As quick a growth to meet Decay,
As you, or any thing.
We die,
As your hours doe, and drie
Away,
Like to the Summers raine;
Or as the pearles of Mornings dew
Ne'r to be found againe.

The concept of change, of decline towards Death, recurs
throughout *Hesperides* :

'To Blossoms'

Faire pledges of a fruitfull Tree,
Why do yee fall so fast?
Your date is not so past;
But you may stay yet here a while,
To blush and gently smile;
And go at last.

What, were yee borne to be
An houre or half's delight;
And so to bid goodnight?
'Twas pitie Nature brought yee forth
Meerly to shew your worth,
And lose you quite.

117

> *But you are lovely Leaves, where we*
> *May read how soon things have*
> *Their end, though ne'er so brave:*
> *And after they have shown their pride,*
> *Like you a while: They glide*
> *Into the Grave.*

The ephemeral beauty of life and nature are confronted by Herrick's keen sense of growth and existence and the transience is made all the more poignant by this strength. At the very second while life has reached its height and beauty is at its full, death is already at work with the process of withering, yet beauty is succeeded by beauty.

Death is constantly waiting for beauty in order to destroy it, and in *Hesperides* the rites of death are always close to the rites of fertility.

The conception of transience is extended into the *carpe diem* theme in the last stanza of 'Corinna's going a-Maying? (see page 135) to produce a startling vision of death.

The theme of *carpe diem* appears in various forms throughout the ages. Long before Horace's time it appeared in Hebrew literature where in contrast to the celebratory attitude of the Greeks and Romans, the idea was deprecated :

1 *For they said within themselves, reasoning not aright,*
   Short and sorrowful is our life;
   And there is no healing when a man cometh to his end,
   And none was ever known that gave release from Hades.

2 *Because by mere chance were we born,*
   And hereafter we shall be as though we had never been:
   Because the breath in our nostrils is smoke,
   And while our heart beateth reason is the spark,

3 *Which being extinguished, the body shall be turned into*
   ashes,
   And the spirit shall be dispersed as thin air;

4 *And our name shall be forgotten in time,*
   And no man shall remember our works;

And our life shall pass away as the traces of a cloud,
And shall be scattered as is a mist,
When it is chased by the beams of the sun,
And overcome by the heat thereof.

5 *For our allotted time is the passing of a shadow,*
And our end retreateth not;
Because it is fast sealed, and none turneth it back.

6 *Come therefore and let us enjoy the good things that* now
are;
And let us use the creation with all our soul as youth's
possession.

7 *Let us fill ourselves with costly wine and perfumes;*
And let no flower of spring pass us by:

8 *Let us crown ourselves with rosebuds, before they be*
withered:

9 *Let none of us go without his share in our proud revelry:*
Everywhere let us leave tokens of our mirth:
Because this is our portion, and our lot in this.[3]

The Greek philosopher Epicurus and his Roman follower
Lucretius stressed the universality, inevitability and the natural-
ness of death and that to fear it would be mere folly. Mental
stress and physical pain were at loggerheads to the real purpose
of life which was to enjoy its pleasures to the full. The Greek
poets, Anacreon and Theognis, the poet of Megara, extol the
virtues of living well, and this attitude is reflected in Herrick's
verse. He writes that 'Borne I was to meet with Age' and that
he will spend his coming hours 'Drinking wine, & crown'd with
flowers'.

He expresses the spirit clearly in his 'Anacreontike' :

Born I was to be old,
And for to die here:

3. The Wisdom of Solomon in the *Apocrypha*, Chapter 2 (1–9) Version
set forth A.D. 1611 Compared with the most ancient authorities and
revised 1894 O.U.P.

After that, in the mould
Long for to lye here.
But before the day comes,
Still I be Bousing;
For I know, in the Tombs
There's no Carousing.

During Rome's 'Silver Age' the enjoyment of the fleeting moment to the full was celebrated by Horace, Tibullus, Propertius, Ovid, Publius Syrus and Seneca. It is in Horace (Book I of the Odes, Ode XI to Leuconoe) that we find the beautiful expression *carpe diem* which represents the theme:

> ... *sapias, vina liques, et spatio brevi*
> *spem longam reseces. Dum loquimur, fugerit invida*
> *aetas: carpe diem, quam minimum credula postero.*

'Live contented, take your glass freely and entertain no hopes of things too distant for so short a life: envious time retires from us the very moment we are speaking: enjoy therefore the present hour, and do not depend upon the morrow.'[4]

Carpere here represents the action of gathering fruits or flowers. The day itself must be plucked, for every day is as a flower that flourishes a short while, and if one delays, it will begin to waste within that very instant of gathering. Latin poets write of this theme in a variety of ways:

– 'Ovid Ars Amoris III' (59–66)

Venturae memores iam nunc estote senectae:
Sic nullum vobis tempus abibit iners.
Dum licet, et vernos etiamnum educitis annos,
Ludite: eunt anni more fluentis aquae;
Nec quae praeteriit, iterum revocabitur unda,
Nec quae praeteriit, hora redire potest.
Utendum est aetate: cito pede labitur aetas,
Nec bona tam sequitur, quam bona prima fuit.

4. Anon translation in *Works of Horace*, London 1811 (2 vols).

*Now already be mindful of the old age which is to come;
thus no hour will slip wasted from you. While you can, and
still are in your spring-time, have your sport; for the years
pass like flowing water; the wave that has gone by cannot
be called back, the hour that has gone by cannot return.
You must employ your time: time glides on with speedy
foot, nor is that which follows so good as that which went
before.*[5]

The Veronan, Catullus (d. 40 B.C.) expresses the idea with
elegance :

V

*Vivamus, mea Lesbia, atque amemus,
rumoresque senum severiorum
omnes unius aestimemus assis.
soles occidere et redire possunt:
nobis cum semel occidit brevis lux,
nox est perpetua una dormienda.*

*Let us live, my Lesbia, and love, and value at one farthing
all the talk of crabbed old men.*

*Suns may set and rise again. For us, when the short light
has once set, remains to be slept, the sleep of one unbroken
night.*[6]

Around A.D. 200 the Athenian poet Philostratus took up the
theme :

'To a Boy'

*Both beauty and the rose have their spring; and he
who enjoys not what is to his hand is foolish; for he
delays among delights that do not brook delay, and in
the face of fleeting joys he loiters. Time indeed is
grudging and effaces the bloom on the flower and
carries away the heyday of beauty. Do not delay at*

5. Translated by J. H. Mozley (Loeb Classical Library).
6. Catullus, translated by F. W. Cornish, Loeb Classical Library.

all, O rose with voice of man, but, while you may and
while you live, share with me what you have.[7]

and in Letter 55 written 'To a Woman' :

. . . and neither Love nor yet roses know
length of time, for this god (Time) is hostile both to
beauty's autumn and to roses' lingering stay. I saw at
Rome the flower-bearers running and by their speed indicating
how precarious is beauty's prime: for their
running signifies that that prime should be enjoyed. If
you hesitate, it is gone. A woman too withers with the
roses, if she loiters. Do not delay, my fair one; let
us join in sport. We will crown ourselves with roses;
let us speed upon our way together.

We can see the nearness of Herrick's 'To the Virgins; to
make much of Time' to Burton's version of the theme. It may
well be that he was shaping into verse a reflection from *The
Anatomy of Melancholy* about the need of fathers to arrange
their daughters' marriages in due time : 'For if they tarry
longer to say truth, they are past date, and no body will
respect them . . . A Virgin, as the Poet holds . . . is like a
flower, a Rose withered on a sudden . . . Let them take time
then while they may, make advantage of youth . . . Let's all
love . . . whiles we are in flower of years, fit for love matters,
and while time serves.'

(Burton's amalgam brings together many classical echoes.)
'Our life is short and tedious, and in the death of a man there
is no recovery, neither was any man knowne that hath
returned from the grave, for we are borne at all adventure,
and we shall bee hereafter as though wee have never beene;
for the breath is as smoke in our nostrils, &c. and the spirit
vanisheth as the soft aire. Come let us enjoy the pleasures that
are present, let us chearfully use the creatures as in youth, let
us fill our selves with costly wine and ointments, let not the
flower of our life passe by us, let us crowne our selves with
rose buds before they are withered, &c Vivamus mea Lesbia

---

7. *Love Letters of Philostratus,* translated by A. R. Benner and F. H.
Fobes. The Loeb Classical Library, Letter 17.

et amemus, &c. Come let us take our fill of love, and pleasure in dalliance, for this is our lot.

"Tempora, labuntur tactisq; senescimus annis." '

Elsewhere in the *Anatomy* Ausonius (*c.* 310–395) is quoted by Burton.

Colige, virgo, rosas, dum flos novus et nova pubes,

'*O maid, while youth is with the rose and thee,
Pluck thou the rose*'.[8]

There is little doubt that these lines must have been seen by Herrick. Burton also quotes the lines of Catullus V with Jonson's translation :

*Sunnes that set may rise againe,
But if once we lose this light,
'Tis with us perpetuall night.*

During the Renaissance in England Spenser, probably influenced by Tasso, who in turn had probably taken his inspiration from Ausonius' lines wrote in the *Faerie Queene* (Book II, Canto XII 75) :

*So passeth, in the passing of a Day,
Of mortal Life the Leaf, the Bud, the Flower,
Ne more doth flourish after first Decay,
That earst was sought to deck both Bed and Bower
Of many a Lady, and many a Paramour:
Gather therefore the Rose of Love, whilst yet is time,
Whilst loving thou may'st loved be with equal Crime.*

Carpe diem also appears in Shakespeare's works. In *Twelfth Night* (Act II, Scene III) the clown sings at the request of Sir Toby Belch the famous love song 'O mistress mine' the second verse of which runs :

*What is love? 'Tis not hereafter;
Present mirth hath present laughter;*

8. Translation Helen Waddell, *The Temper of the 17th century in English Literature.*

What's to come is still unsure.
In delay there lies no plenty;
Then come kiss me, sweet and twenty;
Youth's a stuff will not endure.

Herrick returned to *carpe diem* throughout his work. In

'To enjoy the Time'

While Fate permits us, let's be merry;
Passe all we must the fatall Ferry:
And this our life too whirles away,
With the Rotation of the Day.

Elsewhere, as in 'To Youth' :

Drink Wine, and live here blithefull, while ye may:
The morrowes life too late is, Live to day.

To 'Sappho' :

Let us now take time, and play,
Love, and live here while we may;
Drink rich wine; and make good cheere,
While we have our being here:
For, once dead, and laid i'th grave,
No return from thence we have.

In 'To live Freely' : 'Let's live in hast; use pleasures while we may . . .' and in 'Advice to a Maid' :

Loue in thy youth fayre Mayde bee wise
Ould time will make thee colder
and thoughe each Morneinge newe arise
yett wee each daye growe oulder

Thou as heauen art faire, and younge,
thine Eyes like twynn Starrs shineinge,
but ere an other daye bee sprunge
all theise will bee declineinge.

124

Then winter comes with all his feares,
and all thy sweetes shall borrowe,
too Late then wilt thou shower thy teares,
and I too Late shall sorrowe.

ffinis

Herrick's famous poem 'To the Virgins; to make much of Time' begins :

1. *Gather ye Rose-buds while ye may,*
   Old Time is still a flying:
   And this same flower that flies to day,
   To morrow will be dying.

There is a gay lilt in the verse and the poem only contains a small echo of sadness in contrast to the earlier lines of Ronsard (1524–85) in the fifth poem in 'Poésies pour Hélène' :

Vivez si m'en croyez, n'attendez à demain
Cueilles dès aujourd'hui les roses de la vie.

The double rhyme in the last line of Ronsard's poem and its widely stretched, resounding metre produce a sense of a magnificent and tragic nobility.

Herrick is lighter. 'Old Time' is no more menacing than the metal figure of Father Time taking the bails off the stumps at the top of the scoreboard at Lord's Cricket Ground.

But the poem is a perfect rendering of the thought of *carpe diem* in a neo-classic manner:

2. *The glorious Lamp of Heaven, the Sun*
   The higher he's a getting;
   The sooner will his Race be run,
   And neerer he's to Setting.

3. *That Age is best, which is the first,*
   When Youth and Blood are warmer;
   But being spent, the worse, and worst
   Times, still succeed the former.

4.   *Then be not coy, but use your time;*
       And while ye may, goe marry:
     For having lost but once your prime,
       You may for ever tarry.

The theme had already become a source of inspiration, at worst a convention, throughout Europe. In Italy, the poet scholar and patron, Lorenzo il Magnifico (1449–92):

> *Quant'è bella giovenezza,*
> *che pur fugge tuttavia,*
> *chi vuol esser lieto sia*
> *di doman v'è certezza . . .*

'*How beautiful is youth which yet flies away, Let those who would be joyful be so. Of the morrow nothing is certain.*'

In Spain, Garcilaso de la Vega (1503–36):

> *Coged de vuestra alegre primavera*
> *el dulce fruto, antes que el tiempo ayrado*
> *cubra de nieve la hermosa cumbre.*

'*Gather the sweet fruit from your happy spring before angry weather covers the lovely peaks with snow.*'

This concept of abundant life cheated by time and of time unconquerable itself cheated, if only for a moment, was, then, one of the *leitmotivs* of Herrick's time. In 'Corinna's going a-Maying' the brightness of his ideal landscape is dimmed in the last stanza by the realization of the unendurable brevity of life's pleasures. This poem incorporates the major canon of *Hesperides*.

17 *Corinna*

'*Corinna's* going a-Maying'[1] is Herrick's finest and most sustained poem – perhaps his masterpiece. Its form is succinct and its theme universal : the world of nature and man's place in nature. Herrick introduces many themes into the work, pagan and Christian. Its background, too, is a combination of various elements made up of two landscapes, the English and the Classical. Within these landscapes such figures as Apollo and Aurora blend without discord with very English objects : whitethorn, cakes and cream, wet trees and dewy grass.

The poem may well have been written in Devonshire, for the old custom of decking the porches of houses with sycamore and whitethorn on May Day was very common in the county at the time. Here, too, the old country customs were still widely practised and Herrick incorporated many of them into the fabric of *Hesperides*. There were vestiges of Druidism, surviving to the largest extent on Dartmoor and fairy superstitions and legends of pixies were rife throughout the entire area of this part of England. The Druids celebrated the Festival of Belus or Bel on 1 May when they sacrificed a spotted cow. Such customs, and also those of the Anglo-Saxons like the worship of Odin, were not so far from the minds of the people in this remote area of Britain. Many heathen practices as the making of May fires were very common in the West.

The poem is doubly pagan for in it the paganism of Greece and Rome is joined to a surviving paganism in Britain. The two cultures are not incompatible : they have much in common,

1. Corinna is the name of Ovid's mistress. It is possible that Herrick took the name from the Latin poet. There are echoes of Ovid in the poem, as well as of Catullus and Horace.

127

and it is worth remembering that the first meaning of pagan is a country dweller (L. pāgānus, from pāgus, the country).

The poem could, however, have been written anywhere and Herrick doubtless had many different May Days in mind. The holiday was celebrated everywhere in the kingdom, not the least in London where the principal maypole was raised every year on Cornhill. Herrick, as any other Cockney of the time, had always been well acquainted with the customs and ways of the country.

In Elizabethan England the festival was still generally observed though it was less of a public function than it had been in the Middle Ages and Tudor times. Young men and women of the city left their houses before daylight and made for the meadows and woods around London to return laden with may, hawthorn and the flowers of spring. Throughout England on this day Morris dancers escorted the maypole to the place where it was to be pitched. For the most part the pole was of birch, but in London it was of more durable wood and stood all the year round. Maypoles were eyesores to Puritans and their erection was forbidden by the Long Parliament in 1644, but the custom was never wholly put down and it returned with the Restoration in 1660.

The name of the month of May is generally held to be derived from Maia, the daughter of Atlas, and the mother of Mercury, to whom the Romans offered sacrifices on this day. But perhaps the festival is a survival of the ancient homage to Maia or Flora, the goddess of vernal productiveness.

Maytime in Herrick's day was, as it had always been, a period of abandon and it remained so in later times. The Puritan pamphleteer, Philip Stubbes, wrote of the festival in his *Anatomy of Abuse* (1583), a denunciation of various customs of the time which he considered needed to be abolished :

> Against Maie, every parishe, towne, and village, assemble themselves together, bothe men, women, and children, olde and yong, even all indifferently : and either goying all together, or deuiding themselves into companies, they goe some to the woodes and groves, some to the hilles and mountaines, some to one place, some to another, where

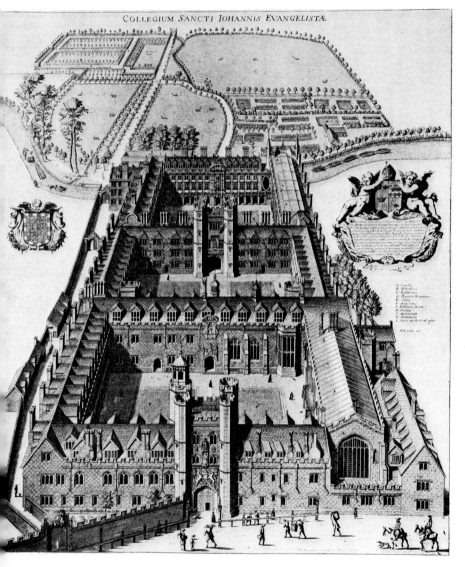

14   *St John's, Cambridge, engraved by David Loggan*

15　The library at Trinity Hall

16　Engraving by M. Merian showing a coach and three of the older type, with a side-seat

17 *An elderly countryman on his nag, engraved by J. Stradanus*

18 *Soldiers loading boats with stores and embarking, engraved by J. Callot*

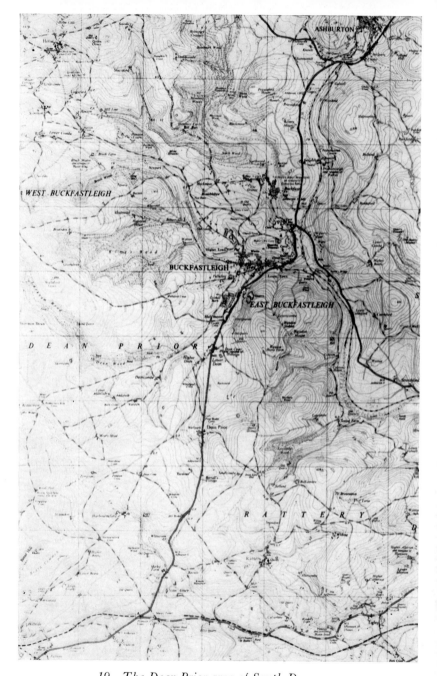

19   *The Dean Prior area of South Devon*
20   *The vicarage at Dean Prior seen from half-way up the large sloping
lawn which, in springtime, is covered with daffodils. The graveyard,
where Herrick lies in an unknown grave, and the church are to the right*
21   *The church and vicarage*
22   *Outhouses at the vicarage*
23   *Dean Bourne, the stream near the vicarage, which Herrick described
as 'rude', possessing 'warty incivility'*

20

21

22

23

24 'Herrick's Walk', the local name for the path which skirts the top of
the sloping lawn of the vicarage
25 The Norman sandstone font which was used by Herrick to baptize his
parishioners
26 The countryside around Dean Prior

27 *Van Dyck's painting of Endymion Porter and his brother*

28 *Portrait of William Lawes*

29   *Ben Jonson*

30   *Rubens' drawing in chalk of George Villiers, 1st Duke of Buckingham*

they spende all the night in pastimes, and in the mornyng they returne, bringing with them birch, bowes, and braunches of trees, to deck their assemblies withall. I have heard it credibly reported and that *viva voce* by men of great gravitie, credite, and reputation, that of fourtie, three score, or a hundred maides goying to the woode ouer night, there have scarcely the thirde parte of them returned home againe undefiled.

All types of people took part in the May Day festivities. They came from all classes and they were both old and young. The maypole was painted, festooned with handkerchiefs, flags, wreaths and ribbons and covered with herbs and flowers. It was drawn by oxen bedecked with nosegays. Women and children followed in its wake.

After it had been raised, straw was laid on the ground around its base. Some people danced and leaped about it and nearby others feasted in the summer halls, bowers and arbours which had been set up.

Throughout his life at this season Herrick must have frequently seen people gathering flowers or dancing around the pole. He no doubt took part in the festivities himself. Somewhere in the back of his mind behind the English celebrations and the classical analogy he seems to have felt something inexplicable and distant.

Like T. S. Eliot writing in *East Coker* of another time of day, but also obscure and half remembered :

> *In that open field*
> *If you do not come too close, if you do not come too close,*
> *On a summer midnight, you can hear the music*
> *Of the weak pipe and little drum*
> *And see them dancing around the bonfire*
> *The association of man and woman*
> *In daunsinge, signifying matrimonie . . .*

and later : 'lifting heavy feet in clumsy shoes' : the dancers move around :

> *As in their living in the living seasons*
> *The time of the seasons and the constellations*

The time of milking and the time of harvest
The time of the coupling of man and woman
And that of beasts. Feet rising and falling.
  Eating and drinking. Dung and death.

There is some distant recollection from his subconscious flickering in the background of 'Corinna' but there is also definite evidence of other sources of inspiration.

Herrick was certainly reminded of the Festival of Flora, the goddess of flowers and gardens, when describing the May scene, for Corinna is compared with Flora (line 17). In Roman times the Floralia lasted in its unbounded licentiousness from 28 April to 3 May. May Day itself was in the middle of the Festival and then the Ancient Romans would go in procession to the grotto of Egeria, the nymph reputed to preside over pregnancy.

'Corinna's going a-Maying' bears an obvious similarity to a shorter poem printed in 1604 in Thomas Bateson's *First set of English Madrigals*, but whether Herrick was influenced by this lyric or not is really of little consequence. His theme is eternal and the amalgam of influences that make up his poem produces a subtle construction of interrelated influences and originality.

The Bateson madrigal is fresh and very charming:

  Sister awake! close not your eyes!
    The day her light discloses:
  And the bright morning doth arise
    Out of her bed of roses.

  See, the clear sun, the world's bright eye,
    In at our window peeping:
  Lo! how he blusheth to espy
    Us idle wenches sleeping.

  Therefore, awake! make haste, I say,
    And let us, without saying,
  All in our gowns of green so gay
    Into the park a-maying.

130

'Corinna's going a-Maying'[1] begins in the usual pattern of an invitation to love. It is a blending of reality and a masquerade, and holds a dramatic quality from the outset:

Get up, get up for shame, the Blooming Morne	1
Upon her wings presents the god unshorne.	2
See how Aurora *throwes her faire*	3
Fresh-quilted colours through the aire:	4
Get up, sweet-Slug-a-bed, and see	5
The Dew-bespangling Herbe and Tree.	6
Each Flower has wept, and bow'd toward the East,	7
Above an houre since; yet you not drest,	8
Nay! not so much as out of bed?	9
When all the Birds have Mattens seyd,	10
And sung their thankfull Hymnes: 'tis sin,	11
Nay, profanation to keep in,	12
When as a thousand Virgins on this day,	13
Spring, sooner then the Lark, to fetch in May.	14

In this stanza objects of nature are identified with things human. From the first line there appears a subtle mixture of three of the main strands that make up the body of the poem : the lines of Humanism, Classicism and Anglicanism. Herrick while celebrating the pagan still does not repress the Christian view.

Line 2 The 'god unshorne' is the bridegroom of Nature, Apollo, the god of fertility himself, towards whom the plants bow in adoration. It is his day which is about to be celebrated. It is also the dawn of the human day and of the growing countryside. 'Unshorne' – the young sun is therefore seen as having locks of hair as beams, a usual classical conception.

Lines 3 and 4 are exquisite, reminding one of the fresh movement of veils in Botticelli's 'Primavera'. All is brightness, early morning light, the morning of youth.

Line 6 Flowers and trees are decorated with spangles of dew like pearls on women's dresses. So Nature is already personi-

1. In addition to my own comments, I have incorporated some of the notes on this poem by L. C. Martin in *Herrick's Poetical Works*, O.U.P; Cleanth Brooks in *The Well Wrought Urn*, Dennis Dobson, London; and S. Musgrove in *'The Universe of Robert Herrick'*, *Auckland University College Bulletin*, No. 38, English series, No. 4.

fied. Aurora has set out before the sunrise, pouring dew on earth to make the flowers grow. Apollo's light will make all vegetation grow further.

Line 7 The dew symbol is continued. Each flower, herb and tree is seen in human terms, a usual device of Herrick. Having wept, they bow like worshippers towards the East – to Apollo. The raindrop/dew metaphor appears throughout the poem. There has been an abundance of rain and moistness. The weather is English rather than classical!

Lines 10–14 The birds sing 'Mattens' and 'Hymnes'. The Christian element enters. The merging is complete. Corinna is accused of being late for the church, the church of Nature. Sin and profanation enter. It is sinful for Corinna to stay indoors.

The second stanza is in part the reversal of the first, for humans are here identified with the spring growth of trees and plants.

Rise; and put on your Foliage, and be seene	15
To come forth, like the Spring-time, fresh and greene;	16
And sweet as Flora. *Take no care*	17
For Jewels for your Gowne, or Haire:	18
Feare not; the leaves will strew	19
Gemms in abundance upon you:	20
Besides, the childhood of the Day has kept,	21
Against you come, some Orient Pearls *unwept:*	22
Come, and receive them while the light	23
Hangs on the Dew-locks of the night:	24
And Titan *on the Eastern hill*	25
Retires himselfe, or else stands still	26
Till you come forth. Wash, dresse, be briefe, in praying:	27
Few Beads are best, when once we goe a-Maying.	28

Lines 15–17 People and houses are decked with foliage on May Day. Corinna has become part of Nature. She has, in fact, become the Roman goddess Flora (Chloris of the Greeks who married Zephyrus, one of the wind sons of Aurora).

Lines 17–24 'Gemms', raindrops/stones: human/nature. *'Orient pearls'* large dewdrops: spring symbols [line 22 'against' = until].

Line 24 'Dew-locks' dew/human. Dew = spring, the early dawn and youth.
Lines 25–27 'Titan' = the sun. The name applied to Saturn by Virgil and Ovid. Originally the brother of Saturn. Titan is not only waiting for Aurora before he can appear. He is also waiting for Corinna.
Lines 27–28 The two religions are in conflict. Corinna is asked to be brief in praying. She moves from the Church of God to the Temple of Nature. The move is natural.
Line 28 'beads' = jewels, and Christian prayer beads.

Come, my Corinna, come; and comming, marke	29
How each field turns a street; each street a Parke	30
Made green, and trimm'd with trees: see how	31
Devotion gives each House a Bough	32
Or Branch: Each Porch, each doore, ere this,	33
An Arke a Tabernacle is	34
Made up of white-thorn neatly enterwove;	35
As if here were those cooler shades of love.	36
Can such delights be in the street,	37
And open fields, and we not see't?	38
Come, we'll abroad; and let's obay	39
The Proclamation made for May:	40
And sin no more, as we have done, by staying;	41
But my Corinna, come, let's goe a-Maying.	42

Line 30 Fields, streets and parks lose all identity. Nature and Man are one.
Lines 32–34 Each house is a part of nature. It is also a temple and a Christian tabernacle. Orthodoxy is assimilated into the Pagan, for Herrick sees pagan rites as Christian rites as well. The village, fully bedecked with greenery, becomes a group of pagan temples, and a grove subordinated to the laws of nature.
Line 41 'sin no more' By the end of this stanza paganism has become triumphant.

There's not a budding Boy, or Girle, this day,	43
But is got up, and gone to bring in May.	44
A deale of Youth, ere this, is come	45
Back, and with White-thorn *laden home.*	46

Some have dispatcht their Cakes and Creame,	47
Before that we have left to dreame:	48
And some have wept, and woo'd, and plighted Troth,	49
And chose their Priest, ere we can cast off sloth:	50
Many a green-gown has been given;	51
Many a kisse, both odde and even:	52
Many a glance too has been sent	53
From out the eye, Loves Firmament:	54
Many a jest told of the Keyes betraying	55
This night, and Locks pickt, yet w'are not a Maying.	56

Lines 43–44 The enactors of the festival have now undergone a partial metamorphosis. As the streets have turned into parks, so the girls and boys have plant-like qualities. They are part of nature; 'budding' = forces of fertility.

Lines 49–50 Youth comes to terms, casually, with Christian customs and the men and women come to the priest to receive the Church's blessing. This is the opposite of the Roman idea. For the Romans the month of May was considered to be unlucky for marriages, since they celebrated the Lemuria, the festival of the unhappy dead, at the same period.

Line 51 'green-gown' O.E.D. – to give a woman a green gown : to roll her in sport, on the grass so that her dress is stained with green.

Sidney : *Arcadia I* (1598) 84 'Then some greene gownes are by the lasses worne in chastest plaies, till home they walke arowe.'

1599 Greene, Geo. *Greene Wks* (Grossart XIV. 140) 'Madge pointed to meete me in your wheat-close . . . And first I saluted her with a greene gowne, and after fell as hard a-wooing, as if the Priest had bin at our backs, to have married us.'

1602 Munday. *Pal. Eng. 11 v* (1639) D. 'At length he was so bold as to give her a greene gowne when I beare me she lost the flower of her chastity.'

Line 52 'Kisse, both odde and even', a country ring game.

Lines 55–56 cf. Shakespeare :

Were beauty under twenty locks kept fast,
Yet love breaks through and picks them all at last.

Venus and Adonis, stanza 96

Until now the poem has been a masquerade set against a pastoral background, a pretence with a backcloth of semi-reality. In the last stanza, however, a serious note appears – the *carpe diem* theme. Herrick here draws from the Apocrypha, the Wisdom of Solomon II, 1–8, from the Old Testament, Proverbs VII, 18, and from Catullus and Ovid, all of which were incorporated by Burton into a passage in 3.4.2.1. (P684) (see page 122). It is possible that Herrick read this passage and was directly inspired by it. This blending of the serious classical theme with the gaiety of the May morning, the juxtaposition of the pagan and Christian religions all add to the force, organization and quality of this poem.

Now the spring morning is over and past :

Come, let us goe, while we are in our prime;	57
And take the harmless follie of the time.	58
We shall grow old apace, and die	59
Before we know our liberty.	60
Our life is short; and our dayes run	61
As fast away as do's the Sunne:	62
And as a vapour, or a drop of raine	63
Once lost, can ne'r be found againe:	64
So when or you or I are made	65
A fable, song, or fleeting shade;	66
All love, all liking, all delight	67
Lies drown'd with us in endlesse night.	68
Then while time serves, and we are but decaying;	69
Come, my Corinna, *come, let's goe a Maying.*	70

Line 60 'liberty' is ambiguous. It implies the release from the flesh when man has finished decaying.

Lines 63–64 Burns knew the poem 'The Primrose' although he did not know Herrick was the author. Whether Burns knew 'Corinna' or not is unknown and very likely he was not influenced by these two lines, but their partial similarity in metre and thought to the following lines in 'Tam O'Shanter' is unmistakable. It might well be that the two poets took similar inspiration from this eternal theme :

But pleasures are like poppies spread,
You seize the flower, its bloom is shed!

> *Or like the snowfall in the river*
> *A moment white – then melts for ever . . .*

Lines 65–68 The poem is now overtly serious though a sad, wistful quality has always been hidden in the background. The poem now tells of the fate of all human-kind and all things transient.

Lines 67 and 68 are akin in their depth to those of other poets of the time, e.g. Marvell's 'deserts of vast Eternity', but so far from Donne's :

> *One short sleepe past, we wake eternally,*
> *And death shall be no more; death, thou shalt die.*

The theme of dew and rain which has again been evoked in *line 63* as representing the vanishing of youth now, in *line 68*, takes on the vastness of dark waters in which all pleasure is eventually drowned.

Line 69 'while time serves' while there is yet time, while time serves us, before we are mastered by time.

There is an ironic element in the idea of *carpe diem*, for love, the subject of all praise and celebration, is no more than an escape from the fate of death, the entry into the abyss of 'endlesse night'. Love resolves nothing, yet it must be pursued. For mankind the moment of pleasure is all part of the passage towards decay, but Flora enjoyed perpetual youth.

The poets who have written on this theme have tended to stand aside from the events or symbols they describe, detached from time, in full control. Herrick is no exception. He may pretend he is Catullus or Ovid, and that Corinna is a pagan nymph, but he remains an onlooker. Corinna is a country girl at Maytime and he a parson.

For the most part Herrick is less of a poet when he has left his ideal landscape or the classical figures that inhabit it. His concept of heaven in 'The White Island' is more that of a prolongation of an earthly paradise ('pleasures' and 'fresh joys') than an affirmation of Christian doctrine. In 'His Letanie, to the Holy Spirit' he really expresses a fear of death, and he also does in 'Eternitie' :

> . . . *Night, shall be*
> *Drown'd in one endlesse day.*

His religious verse has little depth, no intensity, but he can express a personal piety. He is humble before his God and accepts his lot in life with gratitude and simplicity. He is certainly no theologian; after all his studies were mostly in the classics and the law. Most of his *Noble Numbers* are not only lacking in religious interest but they are also dull. There are a few, however, as 'To finde God', that hold some passion and poetry :

> *Weigh me the Fire; or, canst thou find*
> *A way to measure out the Wind;*
> *Distinguish all those Floods that are*
> *Mixt in that watrie Theater;*
> *And tast thou them as saltlesse there,*
> *As in their Channell first they were.*
> *Tell me the People that do keep*
> *Within the Kingdomes of the Deep.*
> *Or fetch me back that Cloud againe,*
> *Beshiver'd into seeds of Raine;*

Tell me the motes, dust, sands, and speares
Of Corn, when Summer shakes his eares;
Shew me that world of Starres, and whence
They noiselesse spill their Influence:
This if thou canst; then shew me Him
That rides the glorious Cherubim.

His religious attitude, is, in general, more of the stoical Englishman inclined to moderate attitudes :

'The Christian Militant'

A man prepar'd against all ills to come,
That dares to dead the fire of martirdome:
That sleeps at home; and sayling there at ease,
Feares not the fierce sedition of the Seas:
That's counter-proofe against the Farms mis-haps,
Undreadfull too of courtly thunderclaps:
That weares one face (like heaven) and never showes
A change, when Fortune either comes, or goes:
That keepes his own strong guard, in the despight
Of what can hurt by day, or harme by night:
That takes and re-delivers every stroake
Of Chance, (as made up all of rock, and oake:)
That sighs at others death; smiles at his own
Most dire and horrid crucifixion.
Who for true glory suffers thus; we grant
Him to be here our Christian militant.

A type of verse in which he is unconvincing is the epigram. In these, for the most part he is obscene without being amusing, critical without subtlety. They are probably placed in *Hesperides* to counterbalance the delicacy of his other verse, sharp reminders of the reality of the country scene of Devonshire in contrast to his own ideal. He can very occasionally show a sophistication which one associates with the eighteenth century, with Pope :

'Upon a painted Gentlewoman'

Men say y'are faire; and faire ye are, 'tis true;
But (Hark!) we praise the Painter now, not you.

and he can display humour too, as in his poem on the Errata of
Hesperides :

For these Transgressions which thou here dost see,
Condemne the Printer, Reader, and not me;
Who gave him forth good Grain, though he mistook
The Seed; so sow'd these Tares throughout my Book.

But such wit is exceptional in *Hesperides*.

He was rather more successful in another genre in which
many poets were trying their skills : the Faerie. The genre had
in fact become a kind of poetic sport.

The realm of the Faerie lay between the human and the
divine worlds and in much of the verse these worlds were interrelated. The Faerie presented poets with a real challenge for
their imagination and only a few could meet it. Shakespeare
alone was completely successful. He revealed this realm in
Mercutio's Queen Mab speech in *Romeo and Juliet* (Act II,
Scene IV) and he reached that point in the topography of
Fairyland which was beyond the attainment of his contemporaries in *A Midsummer Night's Dream* and *The Tempest*.

As a dweller in the 'little world' Herrick could only be
charming in minute detail when writing of a bridal bed of six
dandelion clocks.

Faerie lore grows from such objects as cuckoo spit, toadstools,
dew and gossamer. In the Oberon poems, which were probably
designed to form a fairy saga, Herrick used such symbols with
circumspection and charm, but his vision is restricted.

'Oberon's Feast'

A little Fuz-ball-pudding stands
By, yet not blessed by his hands,
That was too coorse; but then forthwith
He ventures boldly on the pith
Of sugred Rush, and eates the sagge
And well bestrutted Bees sweet bagge:

Gladding his pallat with some store
Of Emits egge; what wo'd he more?
But Beards of Mice, a Newt's stew'd thigh,
A bloated Earewig, and a Flie;
With the Red-capt worme, that's shut
Within the concave of a Nut,
Browne as his Tooth. A little Moth,
Late fatned in a piece of cloth:
With withered cherries; Mandrakes eares;
Moles eyes; to these, the slain-Stags teares:
The unctuous dewlaps of a Snaile;
The broke-heart of a Nightingale
Ore-come in musicke; with a wine,
Ne're ravisht from the flattering Vine . . .

A similar minuteness of vision and fancy is reflected in some of his verse outside the actual genre of Faerie, as in the verses addressed to Mistresse Susanna Southwell, 'Upon her feet' :

Her pretty feet
Like snailes did creep
A little out, and then,
As if they started at Bo-peep,
Did soon draw in agen.

Because of his interest in the Faërie he turned naturally to the folklore of Devon, which provided him with more realistic and arresting models. He observed and listened to the local pagan customs, superstitions and legends,[1] as well as the Christian customs of the time. His Christmas songs cover many of the customs prevailing at Dean Prior such as the Watching of the Pie at Christmas when a solitary watcher guarded the pie throughout the night of Christmas Eve into Christmas Day. The pie represented the manger at Bethlehem and its contents the offerings of the Wise Men.

In *Hesperides* there are a number of popular songs, 'The Hag', 'The Peter-penny', 'Ceremonies for Christmasse', 'Draw

1. As late as 1874, R. J. King recorded in *Studies and Sketches* that the spells, charms and some of the folklore mentioned in Herrick's verse still existed in his parish.

Gloves', 'The May-pole' and 'The Tinker's Song'. Like the poems one associates with this genre, they are pronouncedly rhythmic and melodious. In these Herrick is indebted to the poems of the countryside, and they are in sharp contrast with his lyrics that derive directly or indirectly from the Classics.

He was also familiar with collections of madrigals and miscellany lyrics. 'The mad Maids song', for instance, bears kinship with the madrigals. It is also representative of the preoccupation among the Elizabethans and Jacobeans with insanity, and one is reminded of Ophelia's song in *Hamlet*.

'The mad Maids song'

1 *Good morrow to the Day so fair;*
  Good morning Sir to you:
  Good morrow to mine own torn hair
  Bedabled with the dew.

2 *Good morning to this Prim-rose too;*
  Good morrow to each maid;
  That will with flowers the Tomb *bestrew,*
  Wherein my Love is laid.

3 *Ah woe is me, woe, woe is me,*
  Alack and welladay!
  For pitty, Sir, find out that Bee,
  Which bore my Love away.

4 *I'le seek him in your* Bonnet *brave;*
  Ile seek him in your eyes;
  Nay, now I think th'ave made his grave
  I'th 'bed of strawburies.

5 *Ile seek him there; I know, ere this,*
  The cold, cold Earth doth shake him;
  But I will go, or send a kisse
  By you, Sir, to awake him.

6 *Pray hurt him not; though he be dead,*
  He knowes well who do love him,

And who with green-turfes reare his head,
And who do rudely move him.

7   *He's soft and tender (Pray take heed)*
    With bands of Cow-slips bind him;
    And bring him home, but 'tis decreed,
    That I shall never find him.

Like other lyricists of the period Herrick also took up the theme of the 'Passionate Shepherd to his love', traceable to Ovid's *Metamorphoses XIII* which most likely entered into English poetry through the Italian pastoral. The form and subject had their influence on the song-books of the time. In England these were cultivated versions and the subject was employed as as broadsheet ballad : the counterpart in Scottish literature can be seen in the work of Drummond and in Allan Ramsay's *The Young Laird and Edinburgh Katy*. In this genre Herrick is back in his ideal landscape.

The best known English version, by Marlowe, is borrowed from Greene :

The Passionate Shepherd to his Love

Come live with me and be my love,
And we will all the pleasures prove,
That hills and valleys, dales and fields,
And all the craggy mountains yields.

There we will set upon the rocks,
And see the shepherds feed their flocks,
By shallow rivers to whose falls
Melodious birds sing madrigals.

And I will make thee beds of roses
With a thousand fragrant posies,
A cap of flowers, and a kirtle
Embroidered all with leaves of myrtle;

A gown made of the finest wool
Which from our pretty lambs we pull;

Fair lined slippers for the cold,
With buckles of the purest gold;

A belt of straw and ivy buds,
With coral clasps and amber studs:
And if these pleasures may thee move,
Come live with me and be my love.

The shepherds' swains shall dance and sing
For thy delight each May morning:
If these delights thy mind may move,
Then live with me and be my love.

The Passionate Pilgrim, 1599
England's Helicon, 1600

Answer to Marlowe
(attributed to Raleigh)

If all the world and love were young,
And truth in every shepherd's tongue,
These pretty pleasures might me move
To live with thee and be thy love.

Time drives the flocks from field to fold,
When rivers rage and rocks grow cold,
And Philomel becometh dumb;
The rest complain of cares to come.

The flowers do fade, and wanton fields
To wayward winter reckoning yields;
A honey tongue, a heart of gall,
Is fancy's spring, but sorrow's fall.

Thy gowns, thy shoes, thy beds of roses,
Thy cap, thy kirtle and thy posies
Soon break, soon wither, soon forgotten,
In folly ripe, in reason rotten.

Thy belt of straw and ivy buds,
Thy coral clasps and amber studs,

All these in me no means can move
To come to thee and be thy love.

But could youth last and love still breed,
Had joys no date nor age no need,
Then these delights my mind might move
To live with thee and be thy love.

England's Helicon, 1600

Sir Hugh Evans quotes a version similar to Marlowe's in *The Merry Wives of Windsor* (Act III, Scene I). The theme has remained popular : Keats, Shelley, and later writers have used it for both lyrical and satirical reasons.

The rhythm and the theme were compulsive attractions to many Elizabethan poets. It had great appeal to all ranks in society.

Herrick's poem is entitled 'To Phillis to love, and live with him'. The first eighteen lines run :

Live, live with me, and thou shalt see
The pleasures Ile prepare for thee:
What sweets the Country can afford
Shall blesse thy Bed, and blesse thy Board.
The soft sweet Mosse shall be thy bed,
With crawling Woodbine over-spread:
By which the silver-shedding streames
Shall gently melt thee into dreames.
Thy clothing next, shall be a Gowne
Made of the Fleeces purest Downe.
The tongues of Kids shall be thy meate;
Their Milke thy drinke; and thou shalt eate
The Paste of Filberts for thy bread
With Cream of Cowslips buttered:
Thy Feasting-Tables shall be Hills
With Daisies *spread, and* Daffadils;
Where thou shalt sit, and Red-brest *by,*
For meat, shall give thee melody.

The influence is also clear in 'The Wake' :

144

Come Anthea let us two
Go to Feast, as others do.
Tarts and Custards, Creams and Cakes,
Are the Junkets still at Wakes...

'To the Maids to walke abroad' :

. . . And talke of Brides; & who shall make
That wedding-smock, this Bridal-cake;
That Dress, this sprig, that Leaf, this Vine;
That smooth and silken Columbine ...

and in 'The Apparition of his Mistresse calling him to Elizium'
where the invitation is to die rather than love :

Come then, and like two Doves with silv'rie wings,
Let our soules flie to'th'shades, where ever springs
Sit smiling in the Meads; where Balme and Oile,
Roses and Cassia crown the untill'd soyle.

There is, however, another theme in Herrick's verse which
is far from his idealized world.

19 *His Winding-Sheet*

Humanism had shed grave doubts in the minds of some men. A malaise concerning man's fate and his purpose in living pervaded the thoughts of an educated minority. This was no mere fashion, though for some writers the theme had become a conceit. All men were confronted by such disasters as the plague. Medical care was quite inadequate, diet lacking in fresh fruit and vegetables brought scurvy and left one susceptible to disease. Public executions, floggings, brawling with daggers were, as the bird-picked skulls displayed on London Bridge, constant reminders to the population that death was always near at hand.

Herrick, like Webster, saw 'the skull beneath the skin'. He wrote two dirges and twenty-five epitaphs, and, as we have already seen, the theme of death and transience are threaded into his work. Unease, bred of a dread of death, often serves as a severe undertone to his light-hearted manner. It blends with his love of beauty and zest for life, sometimes confronts love, and it appears in sharp contrast, too, with his most delicate fantasies.

Death is seen by Herrick as the snatcher of pleasure and the final executioner of love. Even Cupid himself is for him love's enemy :

'To Cupid'

I have a leaden, thou a shaft of gold;
Thou kil'st with heate, and I strike dead with cold.
Let's trie of us who shall the first expire;
Or thou by frost, or I by quenchlesse fire; ...

146

Allen H. Gilbert writes in *Robert Herrick on Death* :[1]
'Herrick is hardly to be appreciated unless he is seen to be
aided by two muses, one jocund, the other diviner, inspiring
him to sing of "death accursed; and the victory over death".'
In 'His Winding-Sheet', Herrick reveals some starkly
disturbing conceptions of death as :

> . . . *Where all Desires are dead, or cold*
> *As is the mould:*
> *And all Affections are forgot,*
> *Or Trouble not.*

and later in an imagery acquired from his legal training :

> *The wronged Client ends his Lawes*
> *Here, and his Cause.*
> *Here those long suits of Chancery lie*
> *Quiet, or die:*
> *And all Star-chamber-Bils doe cease,*
> *Or hold their peace.*
> *Here needs no Court for our Request,*
> *Where all are best;*
> *All wise; all equall; and all just*
> *Alike i'th'dust.*

and in 'His Creed' :

> *I do believe, that I must come,*
> *With others, to the dreadfull Doome . . .*

In his profession of clergyman he was naturally a frequent
witness of death, constantly reminded of it and forced to
meditate upon it.

Christianity is a strong component in the work of this most
Epicurean of poets, and 'His Meditation upon Death' is the
kind of work one might expect from a cleric :

> *I'le have in mind my Resurrection,*
> *Which must produce me to that* Gen'rall *Doome,*

1. *Modern Language Quarterly* V, 67 (1944).

To which the Pesant, so the Prince must come,
To heare the Judge give sentence on the Throne,
Without the least hope of affection.

The best of his poems concerned with death are for the most part simple and moving. Children's deaths were common, tragic everyday events in the seventeenth century, and these occurences caused Herrick to write some of his most poignant and delicate verses :

'Upon a child that dyed'

Here she lies, a pretty bud,
Lately made of flesh and blood;
Who, as soone, fell fast asleep,
As her little eyes did peep.
Give her strewings; but not stir
The earth, that lightly covers her.

and again :

'Upon a child'

Here a pretty Baby lies
Sung asleep with Lullabies:
Pray be silent, and not stirre
Th'easie earth that covers her.

This solemn delicacy of tone is reflected too in his epitaphs to grown men and women :

'An Epitaph upon a Virgin'

Here a solemne Fast we keepe,
While all beauty lyes asleep
Husht be all things; (no noyse here)
But the toning of a teare:
Or a sigh of such as bring
Cowslips for her covering.

Herrick's view of death is sometimes Christian, sometimes pagan. He is at his best when confronting it directly with his own particular simplicity and feeling.

20 *Here shall endure thy vast dominion*

ᏨᏫᏫᏋ

Herrick was of course fortunate in being born when the English language was moving from strength to strength. Jacobean English, almost identical to Elizabethan, reached its heights in the Authorized Version of the Bible. This work was now in the hands of the people, artisans, yeomen, tradesmen as well as the ruling classes. It made grandeur and simplicity of expression familiar to most people and engendered a rich and wide vocabulary. Poets found the finest material around them every day, for there existed a delight in inventive speech.

This and a knowledge of the Classics gave Herrick, as any other poet of the time, the perfect means with which to express his thoughts and emotions. Furthermore, despite war and change it was an age when many men still felt their identity was linked to an eternal system and Herrick believed in the earlier Aristotelian world.

S. Musgrove writes in *The Universe of Robert Herrick* : 'The poetry of this century glances from heaven to earth, from earth to heaven with the ease of natural habit, with no sense of effort or embarrassment. It is an age when individual vision and the universal vision coincide, enriching each other in a way peculiarly suited for translation into poetic terms, and with results happier for English poetry than in any age before or since.'

Renaissance England was not only rich in the sources of its culture and in its variety of expression; it was also a period of newness and freshness in the language. Herrick owned this bright quality. 'It is early spring with him', writes Humbert Wolfe, 'The dew is on the grass and the larks are up.'[1] This

1. Preface to *The Poetical Works of Robert Herrick*, Cresset Press, 1928.

freshness in Herrick is aided and heightened by his great skill and subtlety in the use of sounds.

Herrick's scale is not large and his vision is often limited but he is in no way a 'lesser' poet.

Edith Sitwell says of his poems : 'Their form is nearly always suitable to the theme, pleasant and smooth and windless as a summer day; but there is no glory of rhetoric, no supreme line . . .'

Herrick was, it seems, aware of the extent of his vision. Though he produced quite a number of inferior small poems he never created a large disastrous work. He also produced a great variety of verse and there is a unity of purpose – albeit somewhat bedraggled in form in the 1,300 odd poems in *Hesperides* (see page 92). Edith Sitwell assesses him as '. . . essentially a minor poet, and when I say "minor", I do not mean a poetaster (the words "minor poet" have come to be accepted in that sense by the uninstructed) but a poet meant to conceive short, small and exquisite things.'[2] She calls his songs 'exquisite' and 'in their way flawless' but defines their limitation : 'There is no poignant emotion in these poems : all his funeral songs are only for the passing of a honey-bee, dead in the first delicate snows of winter; his bass notes are but the deep droning sound from a hive.'

His attitude towards life was simple, beauty was ephemeral, love capricious, and time the victor, but his work is finished, serene, and his themes universal; added to this he had a keen awareness of metrical pattern and command of an intensely musical and sensuous technique in his use of consonants. At the most superficial level his skill can sometimes appear over-contrived, his feelings to lack any depth at all. John Press remarks on this aspect of his work in his pamphlet *Herrick* : 'when we are satisfied with poems about petticoats or about kissing paps and insteps, we may feel tempted to apply to the girls and mistresses who flit through the pages of *Hesperides* the judgement passed by Millet on Boucher's nudes : that they were not naked women but little things undressed.' And Walter de la Mare in *The Bookman* (1908) writes of this lukewarm quality in his work : 'Herrick's worst drawback, so far as poetry was concerned, seems to have been its freedom

2. *The Pleasures of Poetry*, 1934.

from care, passion or any very acute affliction, failure, or disappointment. He never felt the want of money, or of friends. He enjoyed to the full a long youth, and simply embarked thence into a gay, idle, and convivial manhood.' It is true that in general his work does not reflect passion but it does on occasion show sincerity and expresses that sincerity with a distinct nobility of style. 'To Anthea, who may command him any thing' reflects a conviction in its scansion :

> *Bid me to live, and I will live*
> *Thy Protestant to be:*
> *Or bid me love, and I will give*
> *A loving heart to thee ...*

> *A heart as soft, a heart as kind,*
> *A heart as sound and free,*
> *As in the whole world thou canst find,*
> *That heart Ile give to thee.*

The much anthologized poem of Blakean innocence 'Another Grace for a Child' likewise produces a guilless sincerity :

> *Here a little child I stand,*
> *Heaving up my either hand;*
> *Cold as Paddocks though they be,*
> *Here I lift them up to Thee,*
> *For a Benizon to fall*
> *On our meat, and on us all.* Amen.

Herrick also evokes arresting images :

> *When now the Cock (the Plow-mans Horne)*
> *Calls forth the lily-wristed Morne . . .*[3]

He can recreate everyday occurrences, a scene or event remembered, to transport the reader back to his period in the same vivid manner conjured by Shakespeare in *Love's Labour Lost* :

> *When icicles hang by the wall*
> *And Dick the shepherd blows his nail*

3. 'The Country life, to The honoured, M. End. Porter.'

And Tom bears logs into the hall
And milk comes frozen home in pail . . .

This over-reality can be seen in Herrick's 'When he would have his Verses read' :

When Laurell spirts 'ith fire, and when the Hearth
Smiles to it selfe, and guilds the roofe with mirth; . . .

He can reflect a contented mind with very great beauty :

'The comming of good luck'

So Good-luck came, and on my roofe did light,
Like noyse-lesse Snow; or as the dew of night:
Not all at once, but gently, as the trees
Are, by the Sun-beams, tickel'd by degrees.

Poems such as 'Lovers, how they come and part' hold an all-pervading delicacy and softness :

. . . So silently they one to th'other come,
As colours steale into the Peare or Plum
And Aire-like, leave no pression to be seen
Where e're they met, or parting place has been.

as does 'To Electra' :

I dare not ask a kisse;
I dare not beg a smile;
Lest having that, or this,
I might grow proud the while.

No, no, the utmost share
Of my desire, shall be
Onely to kisse that Aire,
That lately kissed thee.

At times he can be starkly arresting. In a 'Meditation for his Mistresse', having listed flowers comparing their lot to hers (to be withered and 'forced hence') he confronts the reader in the last verse of the poem with the directness of Baudelaire's 'Hypocrite lecteur, mon semblable, mon frère'.

> 7 *You are the Queen all flowers among,*
> *But die you must (faire Maid) ere long,*
> *As He, the maker of this Song.*

In 'To Musick, to becalme a sweet-sick youth', a poem included under songs in W. H. Auden's *A Certain World*, Herrick displays a great elegance particularly telling in his conception of a 'civill Wildernesse of sleep' :

> *Charms, that call down the moon from out her sphere,*
> *On this sick youth work your enchantments here:*
> *Bind up his senses with your numbers, so,*
> *As to entrance his paine, or cure his woe.*
> *Fall gently, gently, and a while him keep*
> *Lost in the civill Wildernesse of sleep:*
> *That done, then let him, dispossest of paine,*
> *Like to a slumbring Bride, awake againe.*

Although the theme is not original (Herrick is possibly indebted to Joseph Hall in his *Meditations*, 1616), the two-lined poem 'Dreames' is succinct and deep :

> *Here we are all, by day; By night w'are hurl'd*
> *By dreames, each one, into a sev'rall world.*

Some of his most perfect verses were written to Julia. Edith Sitwell writes of 'The Night Piece to Julia', a poem whose subtle rhythm is reminiscent of Jonson, that it gives the reader the feeling of 'a lady in rustling silks flying down the midnight branch-shaddowed paths', followed by the firefly–darting sound caused by the much shorter and quicker internal lines :

> *And the Elves also*
> *Whose little eyes glow . . .*

'Upon Julia's Voice' makes use of 's' sounds and a perfect half matching of the words : voice and noise, chamber and amber.

So smooth, so sweet, so silv'ry is thy voice,
As, could they hear, the Damn'd would make no noise,
But listen to thee, (walking in thy chamber)
Melting melodious words, to Lutes of Amber.

Herrick's words are delicate, soft or brittle, but the effect is telling. De la Mare wrote of Herrick's verse in *The Bookman* (May 1908): 'They seem to shed light, these poems, like colourless flowers at evening. A fainter music haunts their sound.'

The most famous and perhaps most perfect of the Julia poems is 'Upon Julia's Clothes':

> *When as in silks my Julia goes,*
> *Then, then (me thinks) how sweetly flowes*
> *That liquefaction of her clothes.*[4]
>
> *Next, when I cast mine eyes and see*
> *That brave Vibration each way free;*
> *O how that glittering taketh me!*

It is a poem open to many interpretations. Louis H. Leiter[5] sees in it a submerged metaphor of 'the angler angled'. The natural element for Julia is her clothing as the natural element for a fish is water; and the suggestion in 'flows' and 'liquefaction' shows that Julia's element by analogy is also water. The angler's vocabulary continues with 'cast mine eyes' and brave vibrations are the movements of a fish. (Brave can also have the meaning of wild, savage or dangerous.) At the moment of drama it is the angler who is fished. Julia catches him: 'O how that glittering taketh me'. To 'take', like 'cast', is one of the angler's stock words meaning to rise to the bait, to be caught. Leiter writes: 'The poem, then, on the level of the submerged metaphor contains a comparison of the angler angling for a fish, hovering, gleaming in the water, with the poet's viewing Julia, flowing, glittering in or out of her silks. The reversal at "taketh me" strikes us with the full force of

4. The old pronunciation is 'cloes'.
5. Herrick's 'Upon Julia's Clothes', *Modern Language Notes* LXXIII, p. 331 (May 1958), Baltimore.

Herrick's sensuous, many-sided, ironic wit : the hunter hunted, the angler angled, the pursuer pursued and captured.'

The poem is a work which can be read in many different ways. The key word is liquefaction. It combines the liquid quality of the silk with the very noise caused by the movement of Julia's dress. A break in the smoothness of the metre of the first line is made by the tiny pause of 'Then, then' and we see the silken clothes held for a second before shimmering in another direction. The metre then flows again as do the clothes themselves. We actually *see* Julia in movement. The flow is first downward and then there is a horizontal shimmering. Each time the poem is repeated we see her movement once more as if looking again at a short sequence from a film of superb quality.

The poems just quoted show Herrick's genius as one of delicacy matched by subtle feeling. Lighthearted but not trivial, they hold an airy brightness, a surface brilliance, and possess the high degree of craftmanship, grace, and the elegant shape of fine glassware. Yet his collected verse does not only represent a showcase displaying many exquisite objects among a few of conventional form. He did more than this. He wrote, albeit lightly, about eternal themes and with a fine sense of balance and artistic poise he created an Arcadian landscape, a new Hesperides, the realm of the setting sun.

155

21 *Glorie*

꩜

I make no haste to have my Numbers read.
Seldome comes Glorie till a man be dead.

Some of Herrick's verse can be dated between 1610 and 1640,
but very little appeared in print before Milton had begun
to dominate the literary scene. Herrick was fifty-seven when
in 1648 he published *Hesperides*. The volume seems to have
brought him little fame, and before its publication, when his
poems appeared in other volumes as *Witt's Recreations* or
song books they did not generally bear his name. His reputation in literary London was at its height in 1625, when aged
thirty-four he was ranked beside Jonson. At this period his
works were for the most part circulated in manuscript.

Herrick was certainly fully confident of his immortality. He
believed that *Hesperides* would not only bring enduring fame
to himself, but also to those friends, acquaintances, and patrons
who were the subjects of poems scattered throughout its pages.
In his own words they became his 'righteous tribe' and gems
'in this eternal coronet'. Each was thus endowed with a monument more durable than 'marble, brass or jet'.

In 'His Poetrie his pillar' he writes :

> *Pillars let some set up,*
> *(If so they please)*
> *Here is my hope,*
> *And my* Pyramides.

and 'On himselfe' :

> *Live by thy Muse thou shalt; when others die*
> *Leaving no Fame to long Posterity:*

156

When Monarchies trans-shifted are, and gone;
Here shall endure thy vast Dominion.

Though apparently sure of his immortality he yet showed some concern about his 'Fame' and addressed poems to his 'detractors', 'critics' and 'soure readers'.

He must have been bitterly disappointed when *Hesperides* was met by a wholly unappreciative audience. The public's indifference was predictable. Not only was his verse written for an earlier taste but his book was published during the Civil War. He lived isolated in Devonshire, far from the literary centre of London. Not only was his style out of fashion, he was also on the side of the defeated. His death in 1674 attracted little attention.

Wood (who is notoriously inaccurate) writes that Herrick's poems 'made him much admired in the time when they were published, especially by the generous and born loyalists'. These readers must have been a small minority.

There is mention of 'Yong Herric' in *Musarum Deliciae* 1655 in 'To Parson Weeks'. (Herrick was then sixty-four.) In *The English Parnassus* 1657 Herrick is quoted but not mentioned, and in *Naps upon Parnassus* 1658 in verses on the Roman poets is found :

> *And then* Flaccus Horace,
> *He was but a sowr-ass,*
> *And good for nothing but* Lyricks :
> *There's but One to be found*
> *In all English ground*
> *Writes as well: who is hight* Robert Herrick

which is hardly complimentary.

Twenty years after publication the 1648 edition of *Hesperides* had not yet been sold out, for Peter Parker advertised it in a list of books printed and sold by him under 'Books of Divinity'.

Milton's nephew, Edward Phillips (1630–96?) in *Theatrum Poetarum*, London 1675, the year after Herrick's death, published a survey of English poets praising Thomas Randolph and William Cartwright, but placed Herrick with a very minor rhymster, Robert Heath : 'That which is chiefly pleasant in these Poems is now and then a pretty Flowry and Pastoral gale of Fancy, a vernal prospect of some Hill, Cave, Rock, or Fountain; which but for the interruption of other trivial passages might have made up none of the worst Poetic Landskips.'

Twelve years later William Winstanley brought out *Lives of the Most Famous English Poets*, London, 1687, and copied Phillip's judgement.

Granger's *Biographical History of England* (1769–74) contained a brief account of him based on Phillips and Wood, and in 1790 three poems appeared in Ellis's *Specimens of the Early English Poets*. Right at the end of the century, in 1796, there appeared a request in *The Gentleman's Magazine* for information on five obscure writers of the 1650s including Herrick. The editor had been working on a history of Leicestershire and naturally knew of the Herrick family. He or one of the staff of the magazine had read *Hesperides* and remarked that Edward Phillips's opinion of Herrick was correct, and praised Herrick's epigrams only – a predictable attitude towards his verse by a critic in the Age of Reason.

Nathan Drake in *Literary Hours or Sketches, Critical, Narrative, and Poetical* in 3 vols 1804, Vol. III, took a positive though restricted view of *Hesperides* in three appreciative articles : 'Of better than *fourteen hundred* poems, not more than a hundred could be chosen by the hand of Taste. These, however, would form an elegant little volume, and would perpetuate the memory and the genius of HERRICK.' He attempts 'to place the neglected merit of this unfortunate band in its proper light'. He adds later : 'They are miniatures, which though occupying a small space, are wrought with perfect symmetry, and glow with the richest tinting.' Barron Field in 1809 recorded that his poems were still surviving by oral tradition at Dean Prior (see pp. 97, 98). During the eighteenth century he was virtually forgotten although some of his poems were known in their musical settings.

At the turn of the century, then, *Hesperides* was beginning to be read again and selections started to appear. In 1810 *The Quarterly Review* said he had been unjustly neglected. This year also saw the appearance of the first volume to be devoted to his poetry since the appearance of his original work – *Select Poems from the Hesperides*, edited by J. Nott, Bristol, which included 284 of the poems. Nott wrote that 'to republish all were unnecessary; many are better withdrawn from the publick eye'.

Robert Southey (great of contemporary fame and now virtually neglected) was, however, an obdurate detractor; he wrote in *Verse by John Jones, an old servant, and an introductory essay on the lives and works of our uneducated poets* (1831): 'Yet we have lately seen the whole of Herrick's poems republished, a coarse-minded and beastly writer, whose dunghill when the few flowers that grew therein had been transplanted, ought never to have been disturbed. Those flowers indeed are beautiful and perennial; but they should have been removed from the filth and ordure in which they are embedded.'

Campbell had included Herrick in *Specimens of the British Poets* (1819) but he too was to accuse him of coarseness. In 1823 in Edinburgh Thomas Maitland produced *The Works of Robert Herrick with a Biographical Note*. The Romantic Revival had by now resuscitated Herrick's verse, and a large number of editions and selections of his poetry followed right through to the Victorian, Edwardian and Georgian periods.

The Victorians, as writers of the present, disagreed about his stature. Some accused him of lack of depth and originality and of obscurity, praised him for his technical skill alone.

A balanced judgement is given by John Dennis in *Studies in English Literature*, published by Edward Stanford, 1883: 'To pass from Spenser to Herrick is to descend from the heights of poetry to a comparatively low level. Herrick lives in the plain, and his beauties are such as belong to a flat country. His verse is often graceful but it is never elevating . . .' Later Dennis writes: 'In the sweetness of some of his verses Herrick is probably unmatched by any poet of his age. He sings, bird-like, without a care, and with a freedom that seems to owe more to nature than to art. But it is the perfection of lyric art to appear artless, and in this respect he has, we think, scarcely a rival.'

He had a large number of admirers. One enthusiast was Edmund Gosse, who recognized 'this wonderful skill and art' and saw him as a consummate jeweller. Most of his observations lack critical judgement. Gosse does, however, pay recognition to Herrick's real lyrical qualities : 'Among the English pastoral poets, Herrick takes an undisputed precedence, and as a lyricist generally he is scarcely excelled, except by Shelley. No other writer of the seventeenth century approached him in abundance of song, in sustained exercise of the purely musical and intuitive gifts of poetry.'

The Reverend Alexander Grossart, who edited *The Complete Poems* in three volumes (1876) understood that Herrick's melancholy was not 'a mere concession to the age' and that he possessed 'a deeper vein of thinking and feeling than is commonly suspected'.

Elizabeth Barrett Browning saw him as 'The Ariel of poets, sucking "where the bee sucks", from the rose-heart of nature, and reproducing the fragrance idealized . . .' (*The Greek Christian Poets and the English Poets*, 1863).

Equally fanciful is J. H. B. Masterman in *The Age of Milton* (George Bell, 1897) : 'Flowers and maidens, songs and sweet scents, and summer days – these are the things of which he loves to sing – with sometimes an undercurrent of sorrow because flowers fade, and summer days cannot last for ever.'

Understanding praise but in an affected style was also given by Richard le Galienne in *Retrospective Reviews*. Austin Dobson, rhetorical in the extreme in the preface to *Selections from the Poetry of Robert Herrick* Sampson Lowe 1882 wrote : 'With Herrick we become spectators of a country-life which time has "softly moulded in the filmy blue" of doubtfullest remoteness, and over which his poetry cast its inalienable – its imperishable charm.' He concludes that he should not explain the contents of the anthology and 'takes leave' of the reader : 'To explain it more fully or more precisely could be to detain him needlessly – nay even discourteously, from the dainties before him. For who but an Ancient Mariner would button-hole a bidden guest where the host is ROBERT HERRICK!' This cult of overpraise which was later to help induce unfavourable reactions to his lyrics in the middle of the present century reached its climax in exaggerated claims for his genius from Swinburne.

In *Studies in Prose and Poetry* (1894) Swinburne eulogizes Herrick as 'the greatest song-writer as surely as Shakespeare is the greatest dramatist', and in his note in *Flower Poems by*

Robert Herrick (1905) – an identical text is included in Pollard's edition of Herrick's works the same year – Swinburne writes of what he calls 'the first great age of English poetry' : '. . . but Herrick, our last poet of that incomparable age or generation, has matched them again and again. As a creative and imaginative singer, he surpasses all his rivals in quantity of good work; in quality of spontaneous instinct and melodious inspiration . . .' again : 'The last of his line, he is and will probably be always the first in rank and station of English song-writers' and : '. . . But how to enlarge, to expiate, to insist on the charm of Herrick at his best – a charm so incomparable and so inimitable that even English poetry can boast of nothing quite like it or worthy to be named after it . . .'

American writers were also discovering Herrick. From the mid-nineteenth century to the present day a number of books and articles have appeared on him, published in the U.S.A. (see Bibliography). One, by Bassett Wendell shared Swinburne's enthusiasm. He wrote of Herrick with a greater sense of proportion but in a no less florid style in *The Temper of the 17th Century in English Literature*, New York, 1904: 'Spenser's verses are like a section of some vigorous tree, pushing its crest skyward; Herrick's are like an exquisite flower, blooming on some little branch so far from the centre of life that its own perfection seems its whole excuse for being. Here growth can grow no farther. The true course of life lies elsewhere. Yet there are moments when one feels content with the flower alone.'

Two years later, in 1906, *The Poems of Robert Herrick*, edited with a Biographical introduction by John Masefield, was published (Grant Richards). Masefield was also an enthusiastic reader of *Hesperides* but was more circumspect. He recognizes Herrick as unique : 'In his "style", his manner, his record of himself, he stands alone. He is the one consummate singer of light, lovely, delicate lyrics.', and : 'His interest is not so much in life, as in the adornments and luxurious refinements of life.'

On the other hand, Masefield considers Herrick a superficial poet, a craftsman lacking a burning intensity.

Herrick was widely read by the Victorians and Edwardians and often accorded a prominence which he did not deserve.

Palgrave in *The Golden Treasury of Songs and Lyrics* (1861) selected seven poems by Herrick, in contrast to one of George Herbert's. Donne was unquoted. (Shelley's verse, in high fashion, was accorded twenty-three poems.) Herrick's poem 'To the Virgins, to make much of Time' had its title suitably changed to one more reminiscent of advice by a mistress to the pupils of a Victorian girls' school : Palgrave entitled it 'Counsel to Girls'.

Palgrave saw that Herrick's classicism and allegory were a film that covered seriousness (Chrysomela : *A Selection from the Lyrical Poems of Robert Herrick*, London 1877 p. xx).

Other Victorians saw him as superficial poet lacking in 'high seriousness' but during the nineteenth century Herrick had at last become an established literary figure.

Arthur Quiller-Couch devoted twenty-one pages (poems 247–275) in *The Oxford Book of English Verse* (1900), the same as for Shelley (poems 605–618), while Donne only received six-and-a-quarter (poems 195–202) and George Herbert five (poems 281–286).

He was also recognized outside England. Taine in his *Histoire de la Littérature Anglaise* (1863–4) wrote : '*Les seuls objets qu'ils sachent encore peindre, ce sont les petites choses gracieuses, un baiser, une fête de mai, un narcisse, une primevère humide de rosée, une matinée de mariage, une abeille, Herrick surtout et Suckling rencontrent là de petits poèmes exquis, mignons, toujours riants ou souriants, pareils à ceux qu'on a mis sous le nom d'Anacréon ou qui abondent dans l'Anthologie. En effet, ici comme là-bas, c'est un paganisme qui décline; l'énergie s'en va, l'agrément commence.*'

Ernest Hale in his selections wrote that Herrick dealt with two of the great themes of poetry, life and death, but reflecting Southey called much of his work a 'poetical pigsty'.

Saintsbury in his introduction to the *Poetical Works of Robert Herrick*, London 1893, recognized that 'It is not easy to find a poet who is in his own way so *complete* as Herrick'.

The number of editions of Herrick's Works, both collected and in selection, was very large : W. Carew Hazlitt, 1869, Grossart, 1876, Pollard (with Swinburne's preface) 1891, Saintsbury, 1893 and Moorman, 1915. Ernest Rhys issued an expurgated edition in 1908, as did Pollard, 1891, which printed asterisks in place of the lines which he considered of dubious morality, but in his introduction to *Herrick's Hesperides and Noble Numbers*, which appeared in the Everyman edition in 1908, Rhys praises his lyrical qualities : 'In all English lyric poetry, there are few to compare with him. You may begin with Tennyson, and count only a score of names backwards, and then reduce the score to a scant half dozen, and still his note is heard, clear, distinct among them all."

The Edwardian era saw the publication of *Robert Herrick, a Biographical and Critical Study* by F. W. Moorman in 1910, and in 1911 *Robert Herrick, Contribution à l'Etude de la Poésie Lyrique en Angleterre au Dix-septième Siècle* by Professor Florès Delattre of the Lycée Charlemagne; a work of scholarly patience originally a thesis. Like other French critics such as Legouis, and unlike some English writers who deplored what they saw as Herrick's lightness, sensuality and at times mere frivolity, Delattre fully appreciated Herrick's delicate qualities : *'Il est doué par contre d'une imagination sensuelle vraiment exquise. Tant qu'il demeure dans le domain des sensations et des sentiments jolis, il est sans rival.'* Legouis in his *History of English Literature* with Cazamian recognized his lighter gifts for their real worth : 'Never again did a poet of the West have so light a touch. The secret seems to be kept by Japan or China.' And : 'He reverses La Fontaine's otherwise just verdict on the English, that they "think profoundly". Herrick thinks, feels, and writes lightly. He touches nothing; he barely skims the surface. For he was without moral sense. He knew only delicate enjoyment, neither satiety, passion, nor remorse. He is the most epicurean of the moderns.'

After the First World War writers were again divided between the appreciative critics like Wendell and detractors like F. R. Leavis. Some of the most perceptive remarks about his poetry during the twenties and thirties were written by other poets : T. S. Eliot, Edith Sitwell and Walter de la Mare and are quoted elsewhere in this book.

Herrick's severest modern critic was F. R. Leavis who maintained in *Revaluation* (1936) that Marvell had a strength that Herrick lacked : 'Herrick's game, Herrick's indulgence, in fact, is comparatively solemn, it does not refer us outside itself. "Let us", he virtually says, "be sweetly and deliciously sad", and we are to be absorbed in the game, the "solemn" rite.' Herrick, wrote Leavis, had nothing of 'alert bearing' and 'crisp movement', nor 'Marvell's familiar wit'. There was a world of difference between Leavis and, say, W. H. Davies : 'The game we feel also as an exercise in the art of verse; we are aware at the same time of an attitude towards that art, and in that attitude we have the presence of Ben Jonson.'

The year before, December 1935, in *Scrutiny* (Cambridge) Leavis wrote : 'Without Jonson behind him what would Herrick (still an overrated figure) have been? The point of the instance lies in the very triviality of Herrick's talent, which yet produced something not altogether negligible (beside him Carew looks like a major poet), Herrick too, in his trivially charming way, illustrates the advantages poetry enjoyed in an age in which a poet could be "classical" and in touch with a living popular culture at the same time.'

In the twenties and thirties, however, writers such as Humbert Wolfe, who prefaced *The Poetical Works of Robert Herrick,* Cresset Press, 1928, were full of praise for him. Wolfe wrote of his 'dazzling freshness'. Other enthusiasts did him a disservice by uncritical overpraise, such as Llewelyn Powys who wrote in the *Spectator* of 21 July 1933 : 'After Shakespeare and Milton it is to Herrick we should turn.'

The preoccupation with Herrick's 'lightness' and thus with the obverse, his lack of profundity, still commands attention from recent critics.

Louis Untermeyer in his introduction to *The Love Poems of Robert Herrick and John Donne,* Rutgers University Press, 1948, writes : 'Herrick is all delicacy and delight; his Muse is appropriately playful and petulant. His greatest protest is little more than a pout.' 'He charms us today not merely by his prettiness but by a kind of mocking purity.' 'Essentially Herrick's poetry is a triumph of tiny significances. Never has a writer done so much with such trivial material. It may be said that Herrick trifled his way from light verse into lasting poetry.'

But present-day writers have recognized him as a poet with some depth and intelligence. S. Musgrove in *The Universe of Robert Herrick*, Auckland, 1950, sees Herrick as absorbing a rich, varied culture, a consummate master of technique and a poet with a seriousness of purpose: 'In truth, Herrick was neither trivial nor a pagan. He was a poet of stature less only than the greatest – a stature comparable to that of Donne or Marvell – and a Christian of the seventeenth century. In a certain sense, he was so considerable a poet just *because* he was a Christian of the seventeenth century. In other words, Herrick, like the other outstanding poets of his time, was an inheritor of that great world system of thought and vision, that hierarchical cosmology which his century had inherited from the middle ages and turned to such splendid poetic use . . .'

L. C. Martin in his Introduction to *The Poetical Works of Robert Herrick*, Oxford, 1968, reflects much the same ideas: 'Better knowledge of Jacobean and Caroline poetry has revealed more clearly what he had in common with other writers and what he contributed of his own. The seriousness expressed or implied in much that he wrote has been brought more fully into light, and it is an advantage also that his work as a whole can now be seen to share in the complexity which belongs generally to Renaissance humanism, with its roots in classical literature, Christian doctrine, and medieval philosophy, symbolism, and superstition; for this composite inheritance, with its stimulating variety and contrasts, probably did more than the example of any single poet, Horace, Martial, or even Jonson, to make Herrick's poetry what it was.'

Herrick today also has his detractors: *The Pelican History of English Literature* dismisses him with some contempt. Hayward in his selection of Herrick's verse in the *Penguin Poets* series (1961) writes that he had a delicate ear and technical mastery but lacked imagination, and is 'perhaps too fluent'. In *A Guide to English Literature* (vol. 3), published by Penguin and edited by Boris Ford, is written: 'Herrick is a poet of charmingly fanciful but simple sensibility. "Corinna's Going a-Maying" is in the sixteenth-century convention, with its mass of flowery imagery and naive medley of classical allusions and colloquial phrases.'

Maurice Hussey in *Jonson and the Cavaliers* writes that his art possesses strength and though there are many compensations in his works, 'the strength was there though it was rarely evoked.'

J. Max Patrick, however, in his introduction to *The Complete Poetry of Robert Herrick*, New York University Press, 1963, writes of this seemingly eternal ambiguity of approach by critics towards his works : 'Some readers attracted by charm have been repulsed by his earthiness and those who savoured this quality were repelled by what they considered his constant insipid daintiness. The 20th century can relish all kinds of poetry.' Patrick concludes his introduction by : 'Herrick's place as one of the greatest English lyric poets is now secure.'

In *The New Oxford Book of English Verse* (1972) Helen Gardner, following her intent not to reject the familiar, has selected some of his well-known verses as 'To Daffadills', but she has also included such poems as 'To the most fair and lovely Mistris, Anne Soame, now Lady Abdie'. Herrick is given a good section within the book, with thirteen poems.

Herrick's poems have been read frequently on the radio and his work and life have been the subjects of many talks by such varied personalities as Edith Sitwell, Wilfred Pickles, Mary Lascelles, Desmond MacCarthy, Charles Brewer and Geoffrey Earle, and an imaginary portrait was written and produced in 1948 by Douglas Clevendon : 'A Parsonage in the Hesperides'. The poet Peter Porter selected some of his verse on Radio 4 on 8 December 1971 in the series *The English Poets from Chaucer to Yeats* and spoke of his 'feather-like lyrics', his melodious qualities and warmth of heart, and stressed Herrick's dependence on technique. The best talks on Herrick were given by Edith Sitwell. On 28 November 1951 she selected two slight but exquisite poems for her Personal Anthology : 'Upon Julia's haire fill'd with Dew' and 'Lovers, How They Come and Part'. Edith Sitwell said of the latter poem that it : 'Transmutes for us the common day, takes an ordinary event of our daily life, and gives it light like a star. The words shine like a star.'

HERRICK IN FICTION

Herrick has been used as a protagonist in Rose Macaulay's rambling novel *They Were Defeated*, which appeared in the U.S.A. under the title *The Shadow Flies*. James Branch Cabell also placed him in a completely fictional situation in his short story *Concerning Corinna* in the collection *The Certain Hour* (John Lane, The Bodley Head, 1931).

POEMS OF TRIBUTE AND PARODIES

A large number of poems have been written to Herrick (including tributes) by Austin Dobson and Edmund Gosse. None are of any real literary merit.

Parodies have been included in collections by L. Untermeyer, *Collected Parodies*, New York 1926, and C. Wides, *A Parody Anthology*, New York 1914. This work includes two : 'To Julia under Lock and Key' by Owen Seaman and 'Song' by Oliver Herford :

> *Gather kittens while you may,*
> *Time brings only sorrow;*
> *And the kittens of to-day*
> *Will be Old Cats to-morrow.*

HERRICK IN TRANSLATION

Poems by Herrick have been translated into German in 1859 and 1910 by A. Ganzmüller and by F. Freilingrath; into French by Legouis in 1893, 1923 and 1925, and F. Baldensperger in 1938; into Danish in 1935 by V. J. van Holstein Rathlou; into Swedish in 1903 and 1917 by P. Hallström, and into Japanese by Shonosuke Ishii, 1971.

Translations into Latin were made by W. Mangin in 1857, and by J. P. Postgate in 1922. In the first translations W. Mangin (*The Fraserian papers of W. M. Redfield*, 1857) includes a Latin rendering of 'To the Virgins, to make much of Time', thus restoring Herrick's verse to its Classical earth.

HERRICK'S VERSE SET TO MUSIC

Herrick belonged to an age when songs were an indissoluble union of music and words. His verse has continued to attract musicians until the present day. His poems have thus constantly been revived to fit the original concept of a lyric.

The following collections of music were set from Herrick's poems during his own lifetime:

I   *Select Musicall Ayres, and Dialogues, For one and two Voyces . . . Composed by John Wilson, Charles Colman . . . Henry Lawes, William Webb . . . London, Printed for John Playford . . .* 1652. Contains 'The Bag of the Bee', 'To the Virgins', 'Among the Mirtles, as I walkt', 'To Anthea', 'The Willow Garland', 'Charon and Philomel', and 'The New Charon'.

II   *Catch that Catch can, or A Choice Collection of Catches, Rounds, & Canons . . . London printed for John Benson & John Playford . . .* 1652 (Hilton). Contains 'On himselfe', 'How he would drinke his Wine', and 'Upon himselfe being buried'.

III   *Select Musicall Ayres and Dialogues . . . London, Printed by T. H. for John Playford . . .* 1963. Contains the same pieces as I except that 'The New Charon' is omitted.

IV   *Ayres and Dialogues . . . By Henry Lawes . . . The First Book London, Printed by T. H. for John Playford . . .* 1653. Contains 'Am I despis'd', and 'The Primrose'.

V   *The Second Book of Ayres, and Dialogues . . . By Henry Lawes . . . London, Printed by T. H. for John Playford . . .* 1655. Contains 'The Bag of the Bee' *and* 'Leander's Obsequies'.

VI   *An Introduction to the Skill of Musick . . . London, Printed for John Playford . . .* 1655. Contains 'To the Virgins' and 'The Willow Garland'.

VII   *Ayres, And Dialogues . . . By Henry Lawes . . . The Third Book. London . . .* 1658. Contains 'The Kisse'. Reissued in 1669 as *Book III of The Treasury of Musick.* See VIII below.

VIII   *Select Ayres And Dialogues . . . Composed by John Wilson . . . Henry Lawes William Lawes . . . And other Excellent Masters of Musick . . . London . . .* 1659. Contains the pieces in I, minus 'The New Charon', and adds 'Not to love' and 'The Primrose'.

Reissued in 1669 as Book I of *The Treasury of Musick.*

IX   *Musick's Delight On The Cithren* . . . *London, Printed by W. G. and are sold by J. Playford* . . . 1666. Contains 'To the Virgins'.

X   *Catch that Catch can: Or The Musical Companion* . . . *London, Printed by W. Godbid for J. Playford* . . . 1667. Contains 'To the Virgins', 'Among the Mirtles', and 'Charon and Philomel'.

XI   *Select Ayres And Dialogues* . . . *By Mr Henry Lawes* . . . *And other Excellent Masters. The Second Book. London, Printed by William Godbid for John Playford* . . . 1669. Contains 'Am I despis'd', 'How Lillies came white', and 'The New Charon'. This is Book II of *The Treasury of Musick.*

Below are listed, in chronological order, musicians who have set Herrick's verse to music. The majority of their compositions are included.

SEVENTEENTH CENTURY

Nicholas *Lanier,* 1588–1666, British
Prince Charles, a Pastorall upon his birth.

John *Wilson,* 1595?–1674, British
Go perjur'd man. See also I and VIII.

Henry *Lawes,* 1596–1662, British
Song: *Whither are all her false oathes blowne?*
Song: *Bid me to live, and I will live.*
The Cooper Smith manuscript contains fourteen poems by Herrick.
In Lawes' manuscript volume there are twelve settings of poems by Herrick. See also I, IV, V, VII, VIII, XI.

John *Hilton,* 1599?–1657, British
Song: *Thou maist be proud.*
Song: *Am I despis'd because you say.*
See also II.

Robert *Ramsey* (flourished around 1630), British
Song: *Go perjur'd man!*
Song for three voices: *Thou maist be proud.*
                    Howle not, you Ghosts and fairies, while I sing.

Charles *Coleman* (flourished around 1636 and onwards. Died between 1662–4) (see I)

William *Lawes,* 1602–45, British
Gather Ye Rosebuds while ye may.
Two versions: (*a*) common time.
              (*b*) triple time.
See also VIII.

Introduction to the skill of Musick eds. 1655, 1660, 1662, 1664, 1666, 1667 etc. See VI

William *Webb* (flourished around 1652), See I.

John *Blow*, 1649–1708, British
Song: *Go perjur'd man.*

NINETEENTH AND TWENTIETH CENTURIES

John *Hatton*, 1809–86, British
To Anthea. A song very popular at the time.

Arthur *Sullivan*, 1842–1900, British
Secular part songs, *Fair Daffodils.*

Hubert *Parry*, 1848–1918, British
Madrigal, '*Fair daffodils*'.
English Lyrics, set VII, No. 5, *Julia.*
English Lyrics, set X, No. 6, *One silent night of late.*
English Lyrics, set XII, No. 2, *To Blossoms.*

Charles *Stanford*, 1852–1924, British
Two part songs: (1) *A Welcome song.*
(2) *To Music.*

Maude de Valerie *White*, 1855–1937, British
Songs: *To Blossoms.*
To Daffodils.
To Electra.
To Music to becalm his fever.

Frederick *Delius*, 1862–1934, British
4 old English Lyrics, No. 3, *To Daffodils.*

Benjamin *Whelpley*, 1864–1946, American
Gather Rosebuds (op. 5).

H. W. *Davies*, 1869–1941, British
Noble Numbers (eighteen poems by Herrick, Herbert and others) for solo voices, chorus, cello and orchestra.

Ernst *Walker,* 1870–1949
Part songs: *To Daffodils.*
To Blossoms.
Song: *Some asked me where the rubies grew.*
Corinna's going a-Maying.

Frederick *Austin*, 1872–1952, British
Let us now take time, for chorus of mixed voices (S.C.T.B.) (unaccompanied).

Gustav *Holst*, 1874–1934, British
Four part songs for mixed voices, No. 3 Herrick: *Her eyes the glow-worm lend thee.*

Fritz *Hart*, 1874–1949, British
Fourteen Songs by Herrick.

Havergal *Brian*, 1876–1972, British
Part songs for women's voices, No. 3 by Herrick: *The Hay* with
orchestra.

John *Carpenter*, 1876–1951, American
Bid me to live.

Roger *Quilter*, 1877–1953, British
Five lyrics for mixed voices:
(1) *Cupid.*
(2) *A Dirge.*
(3) *Morning Song.*
(4) *To Electra.*
(5) *To Violets.*
Five Jacobean Lyrics, No. 3 by Herrick: *I dare not ask a kiss.*
For mixed voices: *Tulips.*
Songs: *To Julia*
        (1) *The Bracelet.*
        (2) *The Maiden Blush.*
        (3) *To Daisies.*
        (4) *The Night Piece.*
        (5) *Julia's Hair.*

Frank *Bridge*, 1879–1941, British
Voice and orchestra, *The Hay,* for baritone.
Song: *Fair Daffodils.*

Arnold *Bax*, 1883–1953, British
Song: *Eternity.*

George *Dyson*, 1883–1964, British
Three Songs of Praise, No. 3 by Herrick: *A Poet's Hymn.*

R. O. Morris, 1886–1948, British
Chorus and orchestra: *Corinna's Maying.*

Albert *Spalding*, 1888–1953, American
Four Songs: *To Daffodils.*
           The Rock of Rubies.
           Cherrie-ripe.
           Song to Musique.

John Tasker *Howard*, 1890–1964, American
Song: *The Primrose.*

E. J. *Moeran*, 1894–1950, British
Choral unaccompanied: *Weep you no more.*
                  Gather ye rosebuds.

Peter *Warlock*, 1894–1930, British
Two short songs:
(1) *I held Love's head.*
(2) *Thou gave me leave to kiss.*

Paul *Hindemith*, 1895–1963, German
Nine English songs, No. 9 by Herrick: *To Music.*

171

Marian *Bauer*, 1897–, American
Fair Daffodils for two sopranos, altos and piano.

Ernst *Bacon,* 1898–, American
Music for two-part chorus of treble voices with piano or organ accompaniment.
First line: The mellow touch of music.

Edmund *Rubbra*, 1901–, British
Five motets, on works of four poets, including Herrick. No. 2 by Herrick: *Vain wits and eyes.*

William *Busch,* 1901–, British
Song: '*The Fairies*'.
Song: '*The Bell Man*'.

Ralph *Wood*, 1902–, British
Six songs: No. 2: *Counsel to Girls,* choral *To Blossoms* for accompanied chorus.

Leslie *Woodgate*, 1902–61, British
A Hymn to the Virgin for baritone, men's voices, strings, piano and organ.
The White Island tenor solo, men's voices, strings, piano and organ.

Robin *Milford*, 1903–, British
Four Heavenly songs (No. 4 by Herrick) for tenor, chorus and orchestra.

Julian *Gardiner*, 1903–, British
Numerous songs by Herrick.

Grace *Williams*, 1906–, British
Song with pianoforte or orchestra: *The Mad Maid's Song.*

Elizabeth *Maconchy*, 1907–, Irish
Song: *A Meditation for his Mistress.*

E. *Carter*, 1908–, American
To Music, for unaccompanied chorus.

Herbert *Murrill*, 1909–52, British
Two Songs Herrick.

Benjamin *Britten*, 1913–, British
Five Flower Songs for mixed chorus, Op. 47. No. 1 by Herrick: *To Daffodils.*
Welcome Maids of Honour in *A Spring Symphony.*

Wilfred *Mellers*, 1914–, British
The White Island for soprano, women's chorus, and strings.

Geoffrey *Bush,* 1920–, British
Voice and orchestra: *Four songs from Herrick's Hesperides* for baritone and strings:
    (1) *The Impatient Lover.*
    (2) *Upon the loss of his mistresses.*
    (3) *To Electra.*
    (4) *Upon Julia's Clothes.*

Ned *Rorem*, 1923–, American
  Flight for Heaven for bass voice and piano.

Sas *Bunge*, 1924–, Dutch
  Four 17th century poems for high voice and piano, No. 3 by Herrick.

Ralf *Greaves*, –1966, British
Song: *The Maypole is up*, voice and piano.

Richard Rodney *Bennett*, 1936–, British
  Epithalmion for chorus and orchestra, *What Sweeter Music* for soprano,
    alto, tenor and bass.

Chronology[1]

Robert Herrick: baptized in London, 24 August 1591
buried at Dean Prior, 15 October 1674

Herrick was born in 1591 in the reign of Elizabeth I, and died in 1674 when Charles II was on the throne. He thus lived through four reigns and the Protectorate, experiencing ejection from his living during the Civil War.

His own life encompassed many events and the entire lives of many of his famous contemporaries. Milton was born at Bread Street a few yards from Herrick's place of birth in Cheapside seventeen years later on 9 December 1608 and he was to die the same year as Herrick (8 November). The greatest painter of the age, Rembrandt, was born and died (1609–69) within Herrick's lifetime.

The year when Herrick was born, Shakespeare (1564–1616) was twenty-seven and had just begun to emerge as a playwright. In 1672, when Herrick was two years from death, Sir Isaac Newton's account of colour experiments was sent to the Royal Society and the scientist had already analysed gravity (1666).

These chronological facts appear somewhat incongruous when considering the life of Herrick, for he tended to live outside the events of his time and remain a man of the Renaissance drawing his inspiration mostly from the Classics during a period of the profoundest change in political life and in literature.

Date	Biography	History	Literature, Arts and Science
1554		Queen Mary I marries Philip, later II of Spain. England reconciled with Rome	
1555		John Knox returns to Scotland from exile in France	

1. Various sources have been used to compile these tables but I am mostly indebted to S. H. Steinberg's *Historical Tables*, Macmillan, 1967, and L. C. Pascoe, A. J. Lee and E. S. Jenkins, *Encyclopaedia of Dates and Events*, English University Press, 1968.

Date	Biography	History	Literature, Arts and Science
1556	Nicholas Herrick (Herrick's father) migrates from Leicester to London to serve his apprenticeship as a goldsmith	Archbishop Cranmer burnt at the stake	Ronsard: *Les Amours de Marie*
1557	William Herrick (Herrick's uncle to whom he was apprenticed as a goldsmith) born. Lived to 95		
1558		Death of Mary I. Accession of Elizabeth I	*c*. Pieter Breughel the Elder: 'The Alchemist at Work'
1559		Elizabeth assents to Act of Supremacy	Titian: 'Diana and Actaeon'
1560		Death of Gustavus Vasa of Sweden	
1561			Francis Bacon born
1562		First Voyage of John Hawkins to West Indies	
1564		Death of Calvin	William Shakespeare born. Christopher Marlowe born. Michelangelo working on 'Rondanini Pietà' to his death this year
1565		Philip II issues religious edict in Netherlands	Tintoretto: 'Crucifixion'
1566		Murder of David Rizzio, favourite of Mary Queen of Scotland	Breughel the Elder: 'The Wedding Dance'
1567		Deposition of Mary Queen of Scots. Duke of Alva sent to the Netherlands	

176

Date	Biography	History	Literature, Arts and Science
1568		Mary of Scotland flies to England. Spanish Inquisition condemns all inhabitants of Netherlands to death as heretics	
1570		Queen Elizabeth excommunicated	
1571		Don John of Austria defeats Turks off Lepanto	
1572		St Bartholomew's Massacre of French Protestants at Paris. Dutch War of Liberation begins	Camoens: *The Lusiads*
1573			Ben Jonson born. Inigo Jones born
1574	Near this date William Herrick apprenticed to his brother, Herrick's father, Nicholas	Portuguese begin to colonize Angola	
1576			First theatre in England opened at Shoreditch
1577		Drake starts his circumnavigation of the world	Raphael Holinshed: *Chronicles*
1578			Nicholas Hilliard, miniature of Elizabeth I
1579		Union of Utrecht	John Lyly: *Euphues.* Spenser: *Shepherd's Calendar*
1580		Philip II of Spain invades Portugal. Proclaimed King.	

Date	Biography	History	Literature, Arts and Science
1580 – *contd.*		Unites colonial empires of Spain and Portugal. Drake returns from Voyage	
1581		Russians begin conquest of Siberia	Cervantes: *Galatea.* El Greco: 'The Martyrdom of St Maurice'
1582	Nicholas Herrick (Herrick's father) marries Julian, daughter of William Stone, a London mercer	Gilbert founded first English colony in Newfoundland	Hakluyt's *Voyages* published
1583			Orlando Gibbons born
1584		Raleigh discovers and annexes Virginia	Palestrina setting of the Song of Solomon in 29 motets
1585		Raleigh begins to colonize 'Virginia' at Roanoke Island (now part of N. Carolina). England openly intervenes in the Low Countries	Shakespeare leaves Stratford for London
1586		Attempt to colonize Virginia abandoned	
1587		Mary Queen of Scots beheaded	*c.* Marlowe: *Tamburlaine*
1588		Defeat of the Spanish Armada	
1589	John Heyrick (Herrick's grandfather) dies aged 76		
1590		Grenville killed in fight of *Revenge* with with larger Spanish force	Sidney: *Arcadia.* Edmund Spenser: *Faerie Queene*, Bks First English paper mill at Dartford I–III.

Date	Biography	History	Literature, Arts and Science
1591	Birth of Robert Herrick 'baptized the XXIIIIth day of Auguste'		Death of St John of the Cross
1592	Nicholas Herrick (Herrick's father) makes will 7 Nov. 9 Nov. falls from upper window of his house and is killed	Presbyterian system established in Scotland	*c.* Shakespeare: *Richard III*
1593			George Herbert born. Izaak Walton born
1595		Widespread rebellion in central and Northern Ireland (lasts to 1603)	Shakespeare: *A Midsummer Night's Dream.* Galileo invents thermometer
1596		English sack Cadiz. England, France and Netherlands ally against Spain	*c.* Shakespeare: *Romeo and Juliet*
1598			Jonson: *Every Man in his Humour* (or 1597)
1599			Shakespeare: *Julius Caesar*
1600		East India Company established	Jonson: *Every Man out of his Humour* (or late 1599)
1601		Essex rebellion. Essex executed for treason	
1602		Dutch East India Company established	*c.* Shakespeare: *Hamlet*
1603		Death of Elizabeth I. Accession of James I (VI). James I grants toleration to Roman Catholics	

Date	Biography	History	Literature, Arts and Science
1604		England makes peace with Spain	*c*. Shakespeare: *Othello*
1605	William Herrick knighted	Gunpowder Plot discovered	Shakespeare: *King Lear* Cervantes: *Don Quixote* (pt. i) Sir Thomas Browne born *c*. Jonson's *Volpone* performed
1606		Edward Coke becomes Lord Chief Justice. Begins to assert that Common Law is superior to the King	Rembrandt born *c*. Shakespeare: *Macbeth*
1607	Herrick apprenticed to his uncle Sir William Herrick	Plantation of Ulster by Scots and English. English settlements in Virginia	Literary partnership of Beaumont and Fletcher (1607–1613)
1608			John Milton born
1609		Moors expelled from Spain	Shakespeare: *Sonnets*. Galileo constructs his telescope
1610	Near this date writes 'A Country Life: To his Brother, M. Tho. Herrick'	Henry Hudson explores Hudson Bay	Jonson: *The Alchemist*
1611	Death of Mary Bond, Herrick's paternal grandmother, at age of 97	Authorized version of the Bible published	Kepler invents astronomical telescope
1612		Death of Robert Cecil. Death of Henry Prince of Wales	*c*. Shakespeare: *Tempest*. Rubens: 'Descent from the Cross'
1613	Herrick enters St John's	Michael Romanov elected Tsar	El Greco dies. Beaumont and

Date	Biography	History	Literature, Arts and Science
1613 – *contd.*	Cambridge as fellow-commoner		Fletcher: *Knight of the Burning Pestle*
1614		Gustavus Adolphus of Sweden captures Novgorod	Napier invents logarithms. Chapman's translation of *Odyssey* (completed 1615)
1615			Cervantes: *Don Quixote* pt. ii (see 1605)
1616		Richelieu becomes Secretary of State	Shakespeare dies. Cervantes dies. Harvey lectures on circulation of the blood
1617	Herrick graduates B.A. from Trinity Hall, Cambridge	Richelieu dismissed. Raleigh's last expedition to Guiana	Van Dyck: 'Study of four Negro heads'
1618	Death of Herrick's uncle, Robert (his godfather)	Raleigh beheaded. Bacon made Lord Chancellor	
1619		Villiers created Marquis of Buckingham	Nich. Hilliard dies. Inigo Jones: the Banqueting Hall, Whitehall (–1622)
1620	Herrick receives M.A.	Mayflower sails for America	Velasquez: 'Water Seller of Seville'
1621		Bacon impeached	Robert Burton: *Anatomy of Melancholy*. *Corante*, first English newspaper (–1641)
1622		Richelieu re-enters Royal Council	Bernini: 'Apollo and Daphne'
1623	Herrick ordained as	Richelieu becomes First Minister (–1642)	First Folio edition of Shakespeare's plays

Date	Biography	History	Literature, Arts and Science
1623 – *contd.*	deacon and priest of the Church of England, 24 and 25 April. 1623–7 Herrick mostly in London, associated with the Tribe of Ben		
1624		Virginia becomes Crown Colony. Dutch colony of New Amsterdam (New York) founded	Hals: 'The Laughing Cavalier'
1625	Herrick writes A Nuptiall Song . . . on Sir Clipseby Crew and his Lady	Charles I accedes to the throne	Bacon: *Essays*
1626		1626–7 unsuccessful expeditions to aid Huguenots at La Rochelle	Sandy's translation of Ovid's *Metamorphoses*
1627	Herrick goes on Expedition to the Isle of Rhé as chaplain to Buckingham	Failure of Expedition to Isle of Rhé	Schütz: *Daphne* (first German opera)
1628	Herrick nominated to the living of Dean Prior in Devonshire.	Petition of Right. Buckingham assassinated	Taj Mahal built at Agra
1629	Herrick's mother dies Herrick appointed to the living of Dean Prior	English settlements in Massachusetts. Charles I dissolves Parliament and tries to rule without it for 11 years	Bernini appointed architect of St Peter's Rome

182

CHRONOLOGY

Date	Biography	History	Literature, Arts and Science
1630	Herrick installed as Vicar of Dean Prior. Writes a 'Pastorall upon the birth of Prince Charles'	Gustavus Adolphus invades Europe	Kepler dies
1631		Gustavus Adolphus defeats Tilly at Breitenfeld. Sir Thomas Wentworth, first earl of Stafford, made lord-deputy of Ireland	Inigo Jones lays out square of Covent Garden market
1632		Defeat of Wallenstein, death of Gustavus Adolphus at Lützen; succeeded by Christina	Galileo Galilei: *Dialogo sopra i due massimi sistemi del mondo* Rembrandt: 'The lesson in Anatomy'
1633		Laud becomes Archbishop of Canterbury	Donne: *Collected Poems* published. George Herbert: *The Temple*. Pepys born. Galileo before Inquisition
1634		Wallenstein murdered. Founding of Maryland. 'Ship-money' first levied	Milton: *Comus* Rembrandt: 'Old Woman'
1635		Second writ of 'ship-money' extended to the whole kingdom	Sir Thos. Browne: *Religio Medici* (pub. 1642). Lope de Vega dies. Foundation of Académie Française
1636		Third writ of 'ship-money'	Corneille: *Le Cid* Harvard College founded as seminary for clergy
1637	Writes: 'Upon Ben Jonson'	1637–38 Ship-money case of John	Descartes: *Discours de la Méthode*

183

Date	Biography	History	Literature, Arts and Science
1637 – *contd.*	(Ben Jonson dies)	Hampden. Charles I attempts to introduce new Prayer Book in Scotland. Outbreak of religious rebellion in Scotland	Milton : *Lycidas*
1638			Descartes invents analytical geometry
1639		Last writ of ship-money	Poussin appointed French Court painter
1640	Herrick in London at or near this date. A volume of poems intended for the press	Portugal becomes independent. Short Parliament. First session of Long Parliament. Stafford impeached by the Commons	Corneille : *Horace* Rubens dies
1641		Stafford beheaded. Massacre of Protestants in Ulster	Van Dyck dies. Claude Lorrain : *The Embarkation of St Ursula.* First mention of cotton goods being manufactured at Manchester
1642		Outbreak of English Civil War	Theatres closed in England until 1660. Rembrandt : 'The Night Watch' Galileo dies
1643	Elizabeth Herrick, Herrick's sister-in-law who kept house for him at Dean Prior, dies	Royalist victories. Solemn League and Covenant between Parliament and Scots	
1644	Herrick writes 'To the King Upon his	Royalists defeated at Marston Moor	Milton : *Aeropagitica* Descartes : *Principia Philosophiae*

Date	Biography	History	Literature, Arts and Science
1644 – *contd.*	comming with his Army into the West'		
1645	Herrick writes 'To the King Upon his taking of Leicester'	Execution of Laud. New Model Army founded. Cromwell defeats Royalists at Naseby. Montrose's army defeated in Scotland	Edmund Waller: *Poems*
1646		Charles I surrenders to Scottish army at Newark	Henry Vaughan: *Poems*
1647	Writes 'To the King Upon his welcome to Hampton Court'. Writes 'To his household gods, Dean-bourn'. Herrick ejected from Dean Prior. Most probably returned direct to London	Scots sell Charles to Parliament	A. Cowley: *The Mistress*
1648	The appearance of *Hesperides*	Cromwell defeats Scots at Preston. Peace of Westphalia	Royal Academy of Arts founded at Paris. Claude Lorrain: *Embarkation of the Queen of Sheba*
1649	Herrick publishes verses on the death of Lord Hastings	Charles I beheaded. England declared Free Commonwealth	
1650		Charles II lands in Scotland. Cromwell invades Scotland. Scots defeated at Dunbar	Milton: *Pro Populo Anglicano Defensio*
1651		Charles II crowned King of Scots. Cromwell defeats	Hobbes: *Leviathan*

Date	Biography	History	Literature, Arts and Science
1651 – *contd.*		Charles at Worcester. Dutch settle at Cape of Good Hope	
1652	Sir William Herrick dies	Dutch found Cape Town. First Anglo-Dutch war begins	Inigo Jones dies. *c.* Marvell: *The Garden* Pascal constructs first simple calculating machine
1653		Cromwell dissolves Long Parliament. Cromwell made Lord Protector	Izaak Walton: *Compleat Angler*
1654		Christina of Sweden abdicates. Treaty of Westminster ends Anglo-Dutch war	
1655		Royalist uprisings. Cromwell prohibits Anglican services	Rembrandt: 'Titus at his desk'
1656			De Hooch: 'A Dutch Courtyard' Jan Vermeer: 'Woman and Soldier'
1657		Charles X crosses frozen sea in winter 1657–8 and threatens Copenhagen	Huyghens designs first pendulum clock. First manufacture of fountain pens at Paris
1658		Death of Cromwell	Hobbes: *De Homine*
1659		The Rump returns to Westminster	Pepys begins his diaries. Molière: *Les Précieuses Ridicules*
1660		The Rump under pressure from Monk, votes its own dissolution	
1660	Herrick returns to Dean Prior	The Restoration. Charles II King of England. Treaty of Copenhagen ends war between Sweden and Denmark	Velasquez dies. Cuyp: 'The Maas at Dordrecht'

Date	Biography	History	Literature, Arts and Science
1661		Coronation of Charles II. Louis XIV assumes absolute power in France	Rembrandt: 'The Syndics of the Cloth Hall'. Molière: *L'École des Maris*
1662		Act of Uniformity (consent to revised Prayer Book). Nonconforming ministers ejected from livings	Royal Society founded. Molière: *École des Femmes*
1663		Royal Charter for Rhode Island	1663–78 Samuel Butler: *Hudibras*
1664		1664–5 Great Plague, 68,000 die in London area. English annex New Netherland	Molière: *Le Tartuffe*
1665		1665–6 Second naval war between England and Holland	Dryden: *The Indian Emperor.* Poussin dies. La Rochefoucauld: *Maximes.* La Fontaine: *Contes et Nouvelles*
1666		Fire of London	Newton analyses gravity. Dryden: *Annus Mirabilis.* Frans Hals dies
1667		Dutch burn English Fleet in Medway. Peace of Breda between England and Holland	Milton: *Paradise Lost.* Racine: *Andromaque*
1668		Treaty of Lisbon. Spain finally recognizes independence of Portugal	Dryden: Essay of *Dramatic Poesy.* La Fontaine: *Fables*
1669			Pepys: *Diary* ended. Rembrandt dies. Racine: *Britannicus*
1670		Hudson's Bay Company founded by Prince Rupert	Dryden appointed Poet Laureate and Royal Historiographer. Pascal: *Pensées*

Date	Biography	History	Literature, Arts and Science
1671			Milton: *Paradise Regained, Samson Agonistes.* Newton constructs reflecting telescope. Leibnitz defines existence of the ether
1672		Third Dutch War. William III becomes Stadholder	Wycherley: *The Gentleman Dancing Master* Newton presents account of his colour experiments to the Royal Society
1673		De Ruyter defeats French and English fleets	Molière: *Le Malade Imaginaire.* Molière dies during rehearsal
1674	Death of Herrick, **15 Oct.**, buried at Dean Prior	England withdraws from war against Holland. Swedes invade Brandenburg and Prussia	Wycherley: *The Country Wife.* Boileau: *Art Poétique.* Milton dies
1675			Rebuilding of St Paul's begun (complete in 1710). Royal Observatory instituted at Greenwich
1677		William of Orange marries Princess Mary, daughter of James, Duke of York	Racine: *Phèdre.* Spinoza: *Ethics* (posthumous publication)
1678		End of Third Dutch War. Popish Plot	Bunyan: *Pilgrim's Progress.* Dryden: *All for Love*
1679		Habeas Corpus Act. New Hampshire created a province separate from Massachusetts	
1680		1680–2 Charles XI transforms Sweden into absolute monarchy	Comédie Française established

188

A Select Bibliography

Collected Works

Hesperides: or the Works both Humane & Divine of Robert Herrick Esq. London. Printed for John Williams and Francis Eglesfield. 1648.

His Noble Numbers or his Pious Pieces. London. Printed for John Williams and Francis Eglesfield. 1647.

[The reason for the discrepancy in the separate dating of *Hesperides* and *Noble Numbers* is unknown. Martin in *Poetical Works of Robert Herrick*, Oxford 1968, suggests that 'the major part of the book could have been printed in 1647 (possibly in two divisions), and the rest, with the main title page, in 1648'.]

There have been a large number of editions of Herrick's poetry both in collected form and in selection. Many of those printed in the late Victorian, Edwardian and the inter-War periods are delightfully illustrated and printed.

Two collections of his verse surpass all others for scholarship and readability of notes and introductions.

The Poetical Works of Robert Herrick, edited by L. C. Martin. Oxford, 1968. Based on the edition of 1648, it also includes additional poems and Herrick's letters to his uncle Sir William Herrick.

The Complete Poetry of Robert Herrick, edited by J. Max Patrick, New York, University Press, 1963. Useful for the reader with little knowledge of the Classics.

Other editions of Herrick's work include :

Select Poems from the Hesperides, edited by J. N. [ott] Bristol, [1810]. The first reprinting of Herrick's verse for over 150 years.

The Works, edited by T. Maitland. Edinburgh, 1823.

Hesperides: The Poems and other Remains now first collected, edited by W. Carew Hazlitt. 2 vols 1869. The first collection to include poems not in the 1648 edition and the first to include letters.

The Complete Poems, edited by The Rev. A. B. Grossart, 3 vols, 1876. Contains an introduction and notes giving information not previously known about the poet's life and his works. Not always reliable.

The Hesperides and Noble Numbers. The Muses' Library, edited by A. W. Pollard, 2 vols, 1891, with a Preface by Swinburne. The second edition, 1898, contains some notes by the Rev. C. P. Phinn, who forbade his name to be mentioned. These notes are inscribed in a copy of Grossart's edition (3 vols) of Herrick now in the British Museum. Phinn's notes have been incorporated in L. C. Martin's *The Poetical Works of Robert Herrick* (see above).

The Poetical Works (Aldine Poets), edited by G. Saintsbury, 2 vols 1893.

The Poetical Works edited by F. W. Moorman. Oxford, 1915.

Biography and Criticism

Aiken, Pauline, 'The Influence of the Latin Elegists on English Lyric Poetry 1600–1650', *The Maine Bulletin*, Feb. 1932. Work of minute scholarship.

Brooks, Cleanth, *The Well Wrought Urn*, Harcourt, Brace and World Inc., New York, 1947. [4th essay 'What does poetry communicate?'] Also Dennis Dobson Ltd., London.

Browning, E. B., *The Greek Christian Poets and the English Poets*, London, 1863. p. 145 : 'Fanciful and rhetorical praise'.

Chute, Marchette, *Two Gentle Men,* Secker and Warburg, London, 1960. Good for biographical details but for the most part lacking in judgement of the man and his work.

De la Mare, Walter, *The Bookman*, May 1908, London. One poet writing about another with imaginative understanding.

Delattre, F., *Robert Herrick: Contribution à l'étude de la poésie lyrique en Angleterre au dix-septième siècle*. Paris, 1912. The best study of Herrick so far this century.

Dennis, John, *Studies in English Literature*, Edward Stanford, 1883. Takes a balanced but perhaps too critical view of Herrick's poetry.

Dobson, Austin, *Selections from the Poetry of Robert Herrick*, Sampson Low, 1882, (Preface), 'Extreme rhetoric'.

Drake, Nathan, *Literary Hours or Sketches, Critical, Narrative, and Poetical*, 3 vols. Vol. III, p. 25. London, 1804.

Easton, Emily, *Youth Immortal*, Houghton Mifflin Company, Boston & New York, 1934. Biography which has dated.

Eliot, T. S., 'What is minor poetry?', *Sewanee Review*, Oct. 1946, 54 : 1–18 [See text and quote]

Field, Barron, *The Quarterly Review* 10 August 1810. Recorded that his verse still survived by oral tradition in 1809.

Frye, Northrop, *Anatomy of Criticism*, pp. 299–301. Princeton, 1957.

Gilbert, Allan H., 'Herrick on Death' in the *Modern Language Quarterly (V)*, 1944, University of Washington Press. Deals with the more serious aspects of Herrick's verse.

Gosse, Edmund, *Seventeenth Century Studies*, Kegan Paul, London, 1883. Praise of little critical value.

Hayward, John, *Robert Herrick*, Penguin Books, London 1961 (Introduction). Writes that Herrick had technical mastery and a delicate ear but was 'perhaps too fluent'.

Hopkins, R. Thurston, *The Literary Landmarks of Devon and Cornwall*. Cecil Palmer 1926. Interesting period piece.

Hussey, Maurice, *Jonson and The Cavaliers*, Penguin Books, London, 1964. (Notes on poems.) Good account of Herrick's poetry, recognizing that art possessed strength (though 'it was rarely evoked').

Judson, A. C., 'Robert Herrick's Pillar of Fame', *Texas Review V* (1920), pp. 262–74. An incomplete account of his reputation through the ages.

King, R. J., *Sketches and Studies*, John Murray, London, 1874, pp. 363–77

Leavis, F. R., *Scrutiny*, Cambridge, December, 1935. Considers Herrick as trivially charming.

—— *Revaluation*, London, 1936, pp. 39–41. In an essay 'The Line of Wit' Leavis denigrates Herrick's verse as self-indulgent and lacking in strength.

Leiter, Louis H., 'Herrick's "Upon Julia's Clothes" ', *Modern Language Notes* LXXIII (May 1958), p. 331, Baltimore, U.S.A.

Macaulay, Rose, Published in England as *They Were Defeated*. Also in America under the title *The Shadow Flies*, New York, 1932. A novel with Herrick as protagonist. Hard going.

McEuen, K. A., *Classical Influence upon the Tribe of Ben*, Cedar Rapids, U.S.A., 1939. An excellent work which devotes much space to Herrick's debt to earlier poets.

Martin, L. C., *The Poetical Works of Robert Herrick*, Oxford, 1968. For introduction (see also under COLLECTED WORKS).

Masefield, John, *Poems of Robert Herrick*, Grant Richards 1906. (Introduction) Praise of Herrick as a light, delicate, but superficial poet.

Moorman, F. W., *Robert Herrick: a Biographical and Critical Study*. 1910. Inaccurate and at times false in its conclusions but has been standard work on Herrick in English since its publication.

Musgrove, S., 'The Universe of Robert Herrick', *Auckland University College Bulletin*, No. 38, English series No. 4, 1950. An important study which maintains that Herrick's poetic inheritance is very diverse and that he is indebted to a wide range of influences rather than to specific writers.

Patrick, J. Max, *The Complete Poetry of Robert Herrick*, New York University Press (The Stuart Editions), 1963. For introduction. (See also under COLLECTED WORKS.)

Press, John, *Herrick*, published for The British Council and The National Book League by Longmans, Green & Co. A useful introduction to the man and his work.

Regenos, G. W. 'The influence of Horace on Herrick', *Philological Quarterly*, XXVI, 1947.

Richards, Irving T., 'A note on the source influences in Shelley's Cloud and Skylark; *P.M.L.A.* 50. June 1935.

Rollin, Roger B., *Robert Herrick*, Twayne Publishers Inc., New York, 1966. An important work of criticism. Very perceptive but the book has a tendency to make the poet's work fit neatly into different theories.

Sitwell, Edith, *The Pleasures of Poetry, a critical anthology*. W. W. Norton & Co. New York, 1934. Is very perceptive and appreciative of Herrick's verse. Intuitive understanding.

Southey, Robert, *Attempts in Verse by J. Jones, an old servant with an Introduction and Essay on the lives and works of our Uneducated Poets*, John Murray, London, 1831, pp. 85–86. Very critical.

Swinburne, Algernon Charles, *Flower Poems by Robert Herrick with a note on Herrick by Algernon Charles Swinburne*, Routledge, London, 1905.

—— Also *Studies in Prose and Poetry* (1894). Extravagant eulogy.

Tannenbaum, S. A. and D. R., *A Concise Bibliography*, New York, 1949. Useful for quarrying into the mass of literature in which Herrick appears, but misleading and in places inaccurate.

Tillyard, E. M. W. and Lewis, C. S., *The Personal Heresy: A Controversy*, Oxford University Press, 1939.

Untermeyer, Louis, *The Love Poems of Robert Herrick and John Donne*, Rutgers University Press, 1948. (Introduction). Argues that Herrick is only a 'light' poet.

Wendell, Barrett, *The Temper of the 17th Century in English*

Literature, New York, 1904, pp. 146–53. Praise of Herrick in a florid style.

Whitaker, Thomas R., 'Herrick and the Fruits of the Garden', *Journal of English Literary History*, XXII (1955), pp. 16–33.

Whitfield, The Rev. J., *Rambles in Devonshire with Tales and Poetry*. Simkin, Marshall & Co., Penzance, 1854. A rather charming account of a visit to Dean Prior during the reign of Queen Victoria.

Wolfe, Humbert, *The Poetical Works of Robert Herrick*, Cresset Press, London 1928 (Preface). A poet's appreciation.

General Index

195

Walker, John, 94
Walton, Izaak, 79
Webster, John, 146
Weekes, John, 47–8, 49, 55, 77, 87(n)
Whitfield, Reverend J., 66
Williams, John, 89
Wilson, John, 54
Wingfield, John, 41

Wingfield, Mercie, 58
Witts Recreations (Minnes and Smith), 77, 156
Wolfe, Humbert, 105, 149, 164
Wood, A., 74, 77, 94, 157, 158
Wordsworth, William, 114, 115

Yard, Lettice, 75

Index of Herrick's Poetry and Works